PRAISE FOR (2P

A MUℒ. ....

Focuses exclusively on the studio craft of the late rap legend

Featuring **EXCLUSIVE INTERVIEWS** with many of his producers, including: Thug Life / Outlawz Member—Big Syke and Napolian and features a multi-chapter interview with Shakur's closest musical collaborator, Johnny J. Offers fans never-before-revealed insight into 2Pac's recording method, songwriting practice and astounding work ethic through marathon 12-hour recording sessions.

IN-DEPTH!! REVOLUTIONARY!! REVEALING!!

Tupac recorded so much material before he died that more Tupac albums have been released since his death than were released while he was alive, **thanks to his mother Afeni Shakur's efforts to keep his memory and music alive.** These posthumous albums include *R U Still Down? (Remember Me?), Lost Tapes 1989, One Million Strong, Still I Rise, Rose That Grew From Concrete, Until The End of Time,* and 2002's *Better Dayz,* along with his one disc released under the Makaveli alias, *Don Killuminati: The 7 Day Theory.* **A prophetic and prolific artist!!**

TUPAC....A HERO to some, A MARTYR to others, and A LEGEND TO ALL!

THE MOST CONTROVERSIAL RAPPER IN HIP-HOP!

—*Vibe Magazine*

EXTENSIVE! POWERFUL! HISTORIC!
TUPAC SHAKUR IN THE STUDIO
...The Studio Years (1989-1996)

TUPAC SHAKUR

(2PAC) In the STUDIO

The Studio Years (1989-1996)

by Jake Brown

TUPAC SHAKUR
(2PAC) In the STUDIO

The Studio Years (1989-1996)

by Jake Brown

Colossus Books

Phoenix
New York   Los Angeles

TUPAC SHAKUR—(2PAC) IN THE STUDIO
The Studio Years (1989-1996)

by Jake Brown

Published by:
Colossus Books
A Division of Amber Communications Group, Inc.
1334 East Chandler Boulevard, Suite 5-D67
Phoenix, Z 85048
amberbk@aol.com
WWW.AMBERBOOKS.COM

Tony Rose, Publisher/Editorial Director   Samuel P. Peabody, Associate Publisher
Yvonne Rose, Senior Editor   The Printed Page, Interior & Cover Design

© Copyright 2005 by Jake Brown and Colossus Books
ISBN#: 0-9767735-0-3

Library of Congress
Catalog-in-Publication Information Pending
2005

Contents

Dedication

This book is dedicated to Tony and Yvonne Rose
for giving me my start in this business, and for continuing
to believe in and take bold chances on me;

to Penelope for being in my life;

and to my late grandparents
Anne 'Nonnie' and Robert Brown…

Acknowledgments:

First and foremost, thank you to the late Tupac Shakur for giving hip hop its soul; to the Shakur Estate, specifically Afeni Shakur for your generous endorsement of our project, and Dina Lapolt and Heidy for your assistance in the aforementioned.

To my publisher, Amber Books, specifically Tony and Yvonne Rose for working as hard as you did to make this book happen in the time frame I gave you to work with; and for continuing to believe in me. I've greatly enjoyed and appreciated our success together over the past 4 years, and this project is certainly my most personal yet, so thank you for doing so much to help bring its fruition about.

To Johnny J for your talent and massive creative contribution to Tupac's legacy and catalog, and specifically, your AMAZING time commitment on this book. You went above and beyond the call in memory of your close friend and collaborator Tupac, and he would be proud.

To Big Syke for your time and insight into Tupac as an artist, philosopher, profit and thug (in the positive—PAClike sense of the word);

and to Napolian for sharing your memories and moments alongside Tupac in the studio and life with us.

Source Thanks: *Vibe Magazine*, QDIII Entertainment, Daveyd.com, Hitemup.com & Steven Makaveli, MTV.com, and anyone else I forgot to mention…

Author's Notes:

While Tupac's legion of fans have been blessed with an average of an album a year posthumusly released since 1997, the fruit of his tireless work, a cottage industry has also emerged out of Tupac's tragic passing almost a decade ago—much of it devoted to sensationalized recountings of his death and the circumstances surrounding it. This industry's main concern has routinely been what many have categorized as the greatest mystery surrounding Tupac's legacy: who was his assassin?

I would argue that this is NOT the greatest or most confounding mystery surrounding Tupac's legacy, rather that conundrum's study ought focus on how any one artist could singularly create such a massive catalog of music, rivaled in creative proliferance perhaps only by Prince? Moreover, in the same time, how that artist could have such a revolutionary impact on the social, artistic, and philosophical shaping of hip hop's broader musical and culture direction—both in his lifetime, and just as potently and provocatively, in the years since?

Even a peripheral attempt at unraveling the latter two questions would take a generation within itself, and when we speak of the legacy of Tupac Shakur, we surely speak in generations. He spoke for a generation through his music, and so in the pages of this book, I have attempted to put aside the preoccupation with focusing on Tupac's death, in favor instead of a focus on his LIFE's work in the studio, where he arguably spent the majority of his time. Those who have participated in—and officially endorsed—the writing and release of this book have done so because all agree that any study of Tupac's legacy should include an intimate and comprehensive study of his recording method; songwriting craft and techniques; collaborative process; artistic personality; his tireless work ethic; and other relevant subject-matter toward the end of answering the question—who was '2Pac in the Studio?' We hope you'll find at least some of those answers in the pages of this book.

—Jake Brown
June 2005

Introduction
Tupac's Legacy

Neo to Zion...
Muhammad to Islam...
Martin Luther King to the Civil Rights Movement...
The Pope to Catholicism...
Aristotle to Enlightment...
Jesus to Christianity...
Ethos to the Universal Soul...
Tupac Shakur to Hip Hop...

Tupac Shakur was a holy being—omnipotent in Hip Hop, the *"Black Jesus."* He spoke for his people in motion picture, lyrical scripture, he paid their price, and died in sacrifice...But for what? Tupac's death was senseless on a human level when considering him "just another young, black male." Still that was his 'Jesus Carpenter', in Tupac's second coming as hip hop's first prophet, he would raise a generation up on his shoulders and carry them to a promised land of Thug Mansions, where fine wine and rhyme flowed plentiful for all who wanted them. Tupac's music was his generation's heaven, and had a sea of followers. He spoke a universal language, spoken in multi-tracked tongues that could advocate for every fight and plight, no matter how contradictory to one another—in a single song. In a historical context, Tupac had to go out the way he did to be considered on the level of any great martyr—be it Martin Luther King, Malcom X, Medgar Evars, and countless others. Tupac's assassination was the first significant loss of a public figure for African-America since that of Malcom X almost a quarter century before. Born in prison literally, raised through the nightmare of poverty, and put through every test in adversity this world had to offer before he'd reached manhood.

Imagine social order changing…Picture deep within the forming of a storm, a people's discontent roaring like a hungry baby's stomach. Imagine a generation crying, starved for social change. Imagine the guilt of a hierarchy exploding at a country club dinner where all the sins of a heavenly-seeming being run naked and raped—by that storm, and only as the first line of attack. An attack for which there is no defense. An attack whose foundation boils with rage, that isn't just trying to survive anymore. A war where pride's translation is sacrifice, in a selfless wave whose crest can't pave over turned-up sand and smooth over two hundred years of slavery. It seems an obvious word, but there is none more clever, in that its aftermath—the emancipation was a doctrine whose truth laid between the lines—which were almost as ugly as the lashes upon the back of our sins. African Americans our history's refugees. Tupac Shakur was their leader by the end of the 20th Century. Any variation of the struggle of blacks in America could look at Tupac and feel like they were gazing in a mirror—whether in a happy moment or a longing one. And he spoke back to them—about everything they needed—as a people—to be proud of collectively, and cautious of individually. Tupac may have seemed like a victim at times, but in his heart it could be argued he was offering merely offering a refuge for those who felt oppression as a part of their every day. His music was a place where they could steal away, the sanctuary that the streets and broken homes and dreams of the inner city would rarely ever be. Tupac's contradictions as a man were natural to his audience, but his precision personally—within his own constitution—would hardly have tolerated such inconsistency. It was his role as an icon to lead all people, of all dispositions, religions, and convictions—to a better day, and he gave his own life for that cause.

Tupac was groomed for greatness through suffering to bring to the mainstream the message that his elders—from Godfather Gerinamo Pratt to Stepfather Mutulu Shakur, to his own mother, Afeni Shakur, all leaders in the Black Panther's Political Party in the late 1960s and early 1970s—had fought, died, and sacrificed their very freedom to set into motion. Any great prodigy must not only embody the teachings of his generations prior, but must also reinvent and reshape that message into its own being to be embraced and embodied by the next generation of students who will one day become its teachers and followers. Of course, any preacher is the most devout of worshipers…He with the most spiritual power typifies the greatest personal piety. But what if the piety of his surroundings—in the context of the ghetto—can only reflect that much more negatively on its prisoners? What if material possessions—albeit few—are the compensation for a shallow self-worth based on the rotten foundation society has provided to not only create, but also reinforce, that contrary self-image. It is then the mission of a people's leader to show them a way out, no matter the immediate cost, and to then show them that the future can only be the future if history does not repeat itself. For history not to be repeated, it must be rewritten in a new dialogue that gives Tupac's people a new sense of value and freedom, based upon equality of both mind, body, soul and MATERIAL and SOCIETAL worth, such that African America in the 21st Century have the same INSTITUTIONAL opportunities as WHITE AMERICA, or LATIN AMERICA.

Tupac's legacy took shape after his death, and though he seemed to live in the moment during his lifetime, the sheer volume of work he was completing behind-the-scenes in the studio to ensure that creative benefaction for his immediate family and larger generation supports the notion that he was aware of his potential to shape a generation, and knew the responsibility he bore therein. To that end, while he had released 4 albums, '2Pacalypse Now', 'Strictly For My N.I.G.G.A.Z.', 'Thug Life Vol. 1' and 'Me Against the World' between 1991 and 1994, as well as approximately 60 unreleased additional tracks, his seemingly indomitable flow was interrupted with a prison sentence, which Pac served between December, 1994 and October, 1995. The circumstances of his first resurrection are now common knowledge in hip hop folklore—Suge Knight posted $1.4 Million bail, and Pac signed a 3-album deal with Death Row Records. When Knight set Tupac free, the reaction from fans was much like the crowd at a racing track when the buzzer first sounds the horses out of the gate, a crazy wind of anticipation and almost simultaneous release. Tupac was hip-hop's thoroughbred, recording an astonishing 150 songs in the eight months between his release from prison and death in Las Vegas. The entire time, Knight was his shadow, and in turn, Shakur in many ways Knight's light. They played off one other brilliantly, as kindred spirits, and as an unstoppable business force, eclipsing the success of any other hip hop artist, or label for that matter, in the history of the genre.

While Tupac was a master at keeping the attention of the spotlight, his ability in the same time to focus on his recording craft has never truly been examined as up close and personally as his thug image was publicly. Tupac knew how to turn any controversy to his advantage, but behind all the shit talking, the rapper worked tirelessly to keep the wheels turning on his very own mini-industry, which in the last eight months of his life would include an average of 3 songs recorded per PM recording session for a total of 150, 2 movies, 8 music videos, countless live performances and media interviews with print and television media, and in the end, $80 Million in revenue generated in one-year from his watershed. Even when Tupac was just 'hanging with the homies' he was working, which was the real secret to his wild success. His work ethic was and remains—with the notable exception of

Jay-Z—unmatched, a fact that even late icon Notorious B.I.G. joked about, recalling that, prior to their beef, "sometimes I would go see Tupac in a hotel and it be like 9 o'clock he'd been done gone in the bathroom to take a shit and come out with two songs. He just wrote with a radio right next to him and some books on the toilet. He was just very talented. And I really hate for some shit like that to flush. The nigga just got caught up and I feel for his family and friends, you know what I'm sayin'. That was a great loss to hip hop."

Tupac had his dedication to the ethic of hard work in common with Suge Knight, and therein, part of what made Shakur's, and in this time, Death Row's presence so intriguing was the inherent lack of stability one felt in their collective midst. Everything had moved so fast for Knight and his camp that no one knew when it would slow down, but felt inevitably the label's beast-like momentum would have to be tamed by something. With Snoop's fate pending in a murder trial that was in its own right a miniature version of what O.J. Simpson's had been, and Shakur's freedom contingent on a successful appeal, Death Row's fate was very much up in the air, though the label continued to rise skyward. Tupac's role in the latter equation was particularly affecting as he openly discussed the possibility of his death as though it were something imminent. The fact that he had narrowly escaped it once before made his dialogue that much more chilling. Snoop once described what he termed as Tupac's knowledge that he was fated to die young: "By the time I started running hard with 'Pac, you could almost see in his face the knowledge he had that death was closing in. A kind of haunted look would come up in his eyes when he thought no one else was looking, a sadness that didn't have a name and was gone as some as someone called him back into the here and now."

Tupac seemed to have accepted that his demise was as inevitable as his rise; that the two went hand in hand. His 'Live by the Gun, Die by the Gun' mentality dictated that Pac's journey was one in which he was prepared ahead of time for the end, seeming to keep it always in sight. Asked by one journalist to describe the title of his Death Row debut, All Eyes on Me, conceptually at the time of its release, Shakur set the tone and pace for what would be his and Death Row's momentum for the next year: "This comes from someone who just spent 11 and a half months in a maximum-security jail, got shot five times, and was wrongly convicted for a crime he didn't commit. This is not from a normal person." Indeed. Shakur was Hip Hop's most sensational figure, and one of its most openly vulnerable. He had the ear of the entire hip hop community, and in the wake of his recent series of tragedies, their collectively sympathy and intrigue: "I learned…on the floor at Times Square (where he was shot 5 times in a robbery)…(that) I don't have any friends, I have family. You're either my all the way family or just somebody on the outside." More importantly, by embracing Knight as his father figure while the nation embraced Tupac's rebirth as an icon, Death Row served as an unlikely catalyst for connecting Tupac with an entire new wave of fans, and for achieving a level of celebrity that, in his peek, was only appropriate. Death Row's single greatest benefit, aside from the tens of millions of dollars that the label took in monthly off of Shakur's album sales, was that the label took on a new identity of its own.

While violence was still an ever-present element of the label's culture, Death Row's presence now spoke for the West Coast, unified in a way that went against the grain of even Knight's age-old gang affiliation. Rather than focusing on gang rivalry, Death Row was finally at the point where it was at the center of a much larger beef that had national implications for the direction hip hop would ultimately head. Sadly, Tupac would ultimately become a martyr of sorts for the label's cause. Tupac's death had a dramatic effect on hip hop as a whole because he was the biggest star the genre had ever seen, and its first true living legend. There was no way around that, for Bad Boy, or anyone competing with him in the year leading up to his death. Tupac had gone out exactly as he had prophesized on his own albums, and the hip hop world, despite the immediate shock of the tragedy, was better prepared for it because Tupac himself

had expected it. As a result, his fans to some degree had become desensitized to the possibility, such that when it happened, the world was somewhat prepared. Tupac was an antagonist, even in his feud with Biggie, where Wallace played more of a defensive, diplomatic position. Tupac expected to die, or at least seemed willing to put his own life on the life for his cause.

By the time of his demise, Tupac Shakur had become hip-hop's John Lennon—its soul. As the personification of a culture's collective angst and hope, Tupac hadn't broken down walls, he had walked straight through them. Adversity was a transparency in the presence of his indomitable spirit and universally appealing charisma. Tupac's work ethic was as legendary as his very existence as rap's first true icon, a position he rationalized as one in which "I got shot five times and I got crucified in the media. And I walked through with the thorns on, and I had shit thrown on me, and I had the word thief at the top; I told that nigga, 'I'll be back for you. Trust me, it's not supposed to be going down, I'll will be back.' I'm not saying I'm Jesus, but I'm saying we go through that type of things every day. We don't part the Red Sea, but we walk through the 'hood without getting shot. We don't turn water to wine, but we turn dope fiends and dope heads into productive citizens of society. We turn words into money-what greater gift can there be? So I believe God blesses us, I believe God blesses those that hustle. Those that use their minds and those that overall are righteous. I believe that everything you do bad comes back to you. So everything that I do that's bad, I'm going to suffer for it. But in my heart, I believe what I'm doing in my heart is right. So I feel like I'm going to heaven."

The fallout from Tupac's death rocked hip hop to its collective foundation, but the latter was also laid for a new industry with hip hop's larger enterprise focused exclusively on the legacy of Shakur, including 10 post-humus albums: '**Makiavelli: The 7 Day The-ory**', '**2Pac & The Outlawz: Still I Rise**', '**Are You Still Down?**' (a **Double CD**), '**Tupac's Greatest Hits**' (a **Double CD**), '**The Rose That Grew From Concrete**', '**Until the End of Time**' (a **Double-CD**), '**Better Days**' (a **Double CD**), '**2Pac: Nu-Mixx Klassics**', '**2Pac Live**', '**2Pac: Resurrection**' and '**Loyal to the Game**'. The bulk of the material comprising the previously unreleased music from aforementioned releases was recorded during the last 8 months of Tupac's life, and resulted in an additional 18 Million records sold within Tupac's larger catalog. As young as hip hop is as an entity, Tupac Shakur will be viewed 50 years from now, when hip hop is 80 + years old, as one of its most scholarly, respected, and influential forefathers. He had, and continues to have, no contemporaries, with the possible exception on some levels of Notorious B.I.G. We don't want our heroes to die, and so we continue to keep Tupac alive through our purchase of his exist-ing catalog, as well as of the volumes of previously unreleased material that continues to emerge from Shakur's archive. The pur-chase of this music is a true celebration of Tupac's legacy, but an a true, focused exploration of the process behind its creation has eluded hip-hop fans until now. We all have read extensively con-cerning the controversy, the circumstances of his death, the con-spiracy theories which have suggested that by the sheer volume of post-humus material, Tupac must still be alive, living in hiding and recording a new album a year for always-hungry fans. As silly as this is, its more romantic than the idea that Pac is truly gone.

In the pages of *Tupac in the Studio*, we will attempt to unravel that myth by becoming students of this prodigy's recording craft—learning what factors from his life outside the studio drove him in the vocal booth; how his always high-powered emotion and pas-sion played into fueling his seemingly endless life-long recording session; the process behind building Tupac's signature multi-tracked vocal style; how his instrumentals were built from the ground up; the atmosphere and rules inside the studio while he was working; how the genius of Tupac's mind could bounce over a plethora of conflicting topic matters in a single song without ever losing

rhythm, energy, or relevance; what it was like late at night when all the liquor was gone, when the weed smoke had cleared the room, when all the thugs had passed out, when all that was left was Tupac and his music—when he could almost surely STILL be found working away at another hit song; and we'll hear this all directly from the producers who worked alongside Pac, from Shock G to Easy Mo Bee to Johnny J, the latter of whom was perhaps Pac's most kindred artistic spirit. Even Suge Knight was impressed from day one of Pac's release at the rapper's tireless work ethic, remarking, according to fellow Death Row Records artist Michel'le that "I remember Suge said 'He's amazing: he doesn't want girls, he doesn't want to party, all this guy does is work!' Pac was always at the studio, whenever he wasn't on a movie or video set, he was at the studio laying down tracks." Frank Alexander, Shakur's former body guard, recollected that "I only saw Tupac... in...the studio...Tupac was quick; he was fast with the pen, the thoughts and the lyrics that just came out of him. It was phenomenal to see this brother at that time doing what he did best and I mean he was putting it down." Fellow rap legend and Death Row label mate Snoop Dogg recalled that "I learned that from my homeboy Tupac, he was a workaholic...He showed me and everybody around us how to focus in on working and being workaholics and doing what we gotta do without time being a factor, just work, without time being a factor. Just get it done, get it situated. If it's a nice album, if you like it to your ear, then put it out, you know what I'm saying. And that's what I learned, there's no such thing as a perfect album. There's such a thing as working and giving the people what they like." While Pac's primary motivation behind his tireless work ethic was making sure his family was taken care of, then and for generations beyond his own, he clearly felt the same love for and from his fans, as they have embraced his catalog with a loyalty and longevity that only per-haps Elvis has commanded in comparable post-humus popularity and record sales. Tupac's legend will run on forever, and while most of his grounds have already been mapped, this is perhaps the one territory in Shakur's massive legacy that has not yet been properly chronicled and documented for fans—past, present, and future. So join us as we delve into the creative inter-workings of arguably hip-hop's Greatest single mind...

Part I:
Shock G and Tupac

1990 —1993

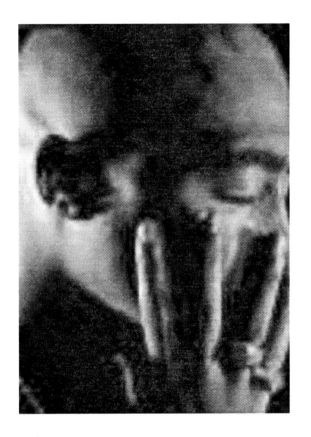

Chapter 1
"2Pacalypse Now"

As a student of hip-hop, Tupac definitely accelerated a few grades. In fact, coming into the game in 1991, not even the most scholarly historian of hip-hop could remember a prodigy quite like Tupac Shakur. The first actor/rapper in the game, Tupac was a living mirror of all that the socio-economic conditions of the inner city produced in the way of the desensitized, the hopeless, hardcore, and hustling products of a ghetto-upbringing generationally, and society's fear of that neglected crisis as it started finally to boil over at the turn of the decade. Tupac was a reaction to the racism of one America, and the battle of another to blend those worlds—at least in context of equality. He was controversy's modern father, and his songs were the rebellious off-spring that inspired a revolution, and entire new genre of rappers in the process. A Renaissance emcee, both Tupac's intellectual and street IQ measured off the map, and he was already re-zoning the ghetto experience for White America with his first album, bringing a new representation and reciprocal acknowledgement of the inner city as it was embodied in the modern-day young, black male. A demographic Tupac reflected in his own image to the most precise detail, he defined the image nationally exactly as he wanted his people to be seen—and most importantly, to be heard. According to Tupac, back in 1991, he saw the problems plaguing the aforementioned demographic as "police brutality, poverty, unemployment, insufficient education, disunity and violence, black on black crime, teenage pregnancy, crack addiction…(In my raps), I show us having the power and in some situations I show how it's more apt to happen with the police or power structure having the ultimate power. I show both ways. I show how it really happens and I show how I wish it would happen...As long as the music has the true to the heart soul it can be hip hop. As long it has soul to it, hip hop can live on."

Tupac's early days in New York, Baltimore, and finally Oakland are well documented. To hear it from Pac's own mouth back in 1991, "I'm from the Bronx, NY. I moved to Baltimore where I spent some high school years and then I came to Oaktown. As for hip hop...all my travels through these cities seemed to be the common denominator...(Tupac is) my birth name and my rap name...(Living in Marin City), you were just given truth to the music. Being in Marin City was like a small town so it taught me to be more straightforward with my style. Instead of being so metaphorical with the rhyme where I might say something like, '*I'm the hysterical, lyrical miracle, I'm the hypothetical, incredible.*' I was encouraged to go straight at it and hit it dead on and not waste time trying to cover things...In Marin City it seemed like things were real country. Everything was straightforward.

Poverty was straightforward. There was no way to say I'm poor, but to say 'I'm po'...we had no money and that's what influenced my style...(I hooked up with Digital Underground and) caught the 'D-Flow Shuttle' while I was in Marin City. It was the way out of here. Shock G was the conductor...The D-Flow Shuttle is from the album 'Sons of the P' It was the way to escape out of the ghetto. It was the way to success. I haven't gotten off since...Basically I bumped into this kid named Greg Jacobs aka Shock G and he hooked me up with Digital Underground and from there I hooked up with Money B, and from there Money B hooked me up with his step mamma, and from there me and his step mamma started making beats. Me and his step mamma got a little thing jumping off. We had a cool sound, but Shock asked me if I wanted a group. I said 'Yeah but I don't wanna group with Money B's step momma 'cause she's gonna try and take all the profits. She wants to go out there and be like the group 'Hoes with Attitude', but I was like 'Naw I wanna be more serious and represent the young black male'. So Shock says we gotta get rid of Money B's step mamma. So we went to San Quentin [prison] and ditched her in the 'Scared Straight' program. After that, Shock put me in the studio and it was on. This is a true story so don't say anything.. It's a true story."

Shock G, for his part, recalls his meeting Tupac as something close to witnessing a miracle evolving, remembering that the young prodigy set what would become the tone for his career in the studio in his first meeting, such that "Layla sent this kid Pac to the studio. We were mixing down 'Sex Packets', (Digital Underground's) first album. Pac came in the studio strictly business—maintained eye contact with me the whole time. I'm at the mixing board, Pac: 'You want me to rhyme now? Sup? Shock G? Sup, I'm Tupac? You want to hear it right now?' I was like 'Damn, this cat's intense.' So I was like 'Yo, run this back, and put some reverb on that track, and we'll go in the booth with this cat.' So we go in the piano, and he busted—and he was street, and educated, and articulate. We came out the booth, and I was like 'Yeah, that was tight.'…In 1990, you weren't really blown away by Pac's rhymes. His rhymes were better than average…It was hip-hop fantasy type stuff, either that or political. It wasn't thugged out yet…As we got to know him, we started working him into the rhyming situations more and more as most we could. We were on our second album at the time, 'E.P. Release', and Dan Akroyd wanted us to do a movie with him—'Nothing but Trouble'—do the soundtrack. And Pac was on tour with us when we got offered that. That's how Pac ended up on 'Same Song.'"

By the time Shock G started working with Tupac on the making of the rapper's solo debut, what Shakur—in the producer's opinion—was still developing in terms of depth of content and perhaps quality—Tupac was certainly making up for in terms of quantity.

Additionally impressive to the volume of work Tupac began amassing from an early point in his career was the process through which he laid his vocals, averaging 3-4 vocal tracks per SONG, a first for any hip hop artist to date at that time. Tupac would go on to make this his signature, but its metamorphosis, as Shock G explained it, began with "Pac (saying) 'I gotta get this shit off my chest, whether it comes out (in stores) or not.' That's why he had stacks of poetry that was his vent, his air, his oxygen. (If he didn't like it), he would just scrap it and do a new song. He just poured it out, more like a jazz improvisationalist. He came in there and said it how he felt it, and he'd be gasping for air, a joint in his hand. Smoking weed and Newports all night, missing words here and there. So the way he would do it, was like the dotted-line principle. When he would gasp for air and miss a line, he'd put it on the next track, and maybe he caught that word. So he would triple his vocals to make sure every word was said.' "

Elaborating on Tupac's early writing/recording style during the 2Pacalypse Now period in his career, fellow Digital Underground member and producer Money B explained that another element of Tupac's creative process which drove his recording pace was simply that "when something happened to him, he wanted to write about it, right there on the spot. Then he'd write it, and go 'Hey, how this sound?' And usually when you say your raps, you're kinda saying your rhymes and figurin' it out. Right after he wrote it, he'd say it just as loud and passionate as if he in the booth. He'd be sweating, spittin'…(then he'd lay it down.)" Even more impressive given the precision of his work method was the fact that, as producer Shock G remembers it, "(In the studio, Pac) couldn't function sober, he didn't like to anyway. There had to be some weed there, had to be some Hennessey, had to be some drink. Had to be something going on." Elaborating on the latter, Tupac for his part explained that "every other record that (I) did, I did high or drunk in the studio while they were making it, laying the beat down. That's why it sounded sloppy, but…I'd be like 'Fuck it, I

feel as though niggaz drunk and high when they listenin' to it."
Tupac's first solo album, '2Pacalypse Now', was released in
November, 1991, right as his first movie, Juice, was released. His
portrayal of the movie's lead character, Bishop, was a mirror for
the all the angst, misdirected passion, and provocative confliction
of the young black male at a time when hip hop had first given the
latter demographic a public identity and platform that wasn't
defined by Reganomics or the 11 o'clock news. Tupac wasn't just
contributing to—but in many ways, entirely writing—the legacy
of hip hop culture as he went along. Perhaps only Ice Cube had as
equally powerful and accurate a perspective and voice as a role
model for the inner city in 1991, and with 2Pac's debut album, he
sought to start the next revolution for black America, explaining
at the time that "the concept (for '2Pacalypse Now') is the young
Black male. Everybody's been talkin' about it but now it's not
important. It's like we just skipped over it. It's no longer a fad to be
down for the young Black male. Everybody wants to go past. Like
the gangster stuff, it just got exploited. This was just like back in
the days with the movies. Everybody did their little gunshots and
their hand grenades and blew up stuff and moved on. Now everybody's doing rap songs with the singing in it.. I'm still down for
the young Black male. I'm gonna stay until things get better. So it's
all about addressing the problems that we face in everyday society...I co-produced it with the members of the Underground
Railroad which is Shock G, Money B, Raw Fusion, Pee Wee,
(and) Stretch from the Live Squad."

Chapter 2
'Strictly 4 My N.I.G.G.A.Z.'

The success of 'Juice' launched Tupac into stardom, landing him a co-leading role alongside Janet Jackson in 'Poetic Justice', John Singleton's follow-up to his own highly successful debut, 'Boyz in the Hood', which had starred N.W.A. co-founder and arguably one of the only other emcees on Tupac's level in terms of popularity and artistic credibility—Ice Cube. Aside from Ice Cube and Tupac, only one other rapper—a veteran of the game, referred popularly to as 'O.G.' or the 'Original Gangsta', Ice T—had also broke onto the big screen via a star-making turn in 'New Jack City', released the same year as 'Juice' and 'Boyz in the Hood.' The club of rapper-turned-actors was a small one, consisting primarily and most-popularly of Ice Cube, Ice T, and Tupac, who—as a trio—also appeared together on a cut from Tupac's sophomore album, 'Strictly 4 My N.I.G.G.A.Z.', which would also become his first platinum album. This certification came in partial thanks to the smash singles 'I Get Around', and 'Keep Ya Head Up' which built upon a theme Tupac had pioneered with 'Brenda Has a Baby', a popular single off his first album which spoke up for the first time in rhyme for the unsung generation of single, black FEMALES who also listened to rap as avidly as did its inner-city male demographic. With 'Keep Ya Head Up', the second single off his sophomore album—and his first Gold-selling single—Tupac would corner the market entirely on male rapper rapping authentically and sincerely for females. An ironic sex symbol in that he retained complete respect in the streets with his male listeners, Tupac was offering something hip-hop had NEVER considered with the lyrics in 'Keep Ya Head Up'—respect for FEMALES. As often as male rappers had talked negatively about their absentee fathers in rap after rap, rarely was equal praise heard for the single mothers who had made up for that absence—playing both parental roles, past a line here or there. Tupac was the first rapper to fill that void with 'Keep Ya Head Up', which swelled the heart of female black America for the first time. Perhaps the greatest accomplishment Tupac achieved with his first cross-over hit was showing his peers and growing legions of fans—specifically males—that it was acceptable to show a softer side amid the hardened exterior required on the block. Future Thug Life/Outlawz member Big Syke explained the latter more specifically, explaining that "Pac was the first cat as a rapper I ever seen put emotions down on paper. I ain't have no rapper write a song that made me wanna cry till I met Pac."

The album's biggest single—and Tupac's first club hit—was 'I Get Around', which Shock G produced for Tupac. As the producer recalls the song's evolution, the instrumental was originally meant for a Digital Underground album, beginning in the "summer of '92...(when) we used to drive around—everybody in the group had a copy of the 'I Get Around' beat—before we wound up giving that to Tupac. That was supposed to be Digital Underground featuring Tupac for the *Poetic Justice* soundtrack. 'Cause 'Pac was working on that movie. But, we make the beats at home, you know, and then we got at least DAT machines at home. We mix them down to DAT, and then bump 'em, and 'I Get Around.' Whooo! The way we made it at home, it didn't need a studio. We wanted to take the two track digital audio tape down, and just add vocals to it...(We) remade it in the studio anyway. And it did lose a little of the crispness. Something about that first take we used to ride around and listen to was crisper and brighter. It wasn't as dull. It was still chunky, but it was more like Timbaland, like digitally crisp, tinny, like metallic. And when we got it in the Starlight

Sound in Richmond (CA) it dulled it a little bit…but it was still chunky. You know, people still felt it…We wound up missing that sound track. 'Cause John Singleton, the director, said he got enough stuff, and we missed the deadline. So then here it is now, like August, 'Pac's album was slated to come out in September. The next Digital Underground album, which was going to be called *The Body Hat Syndrome* wasn't due 'til January. We knew we had a beat that was hot, we wanted it out. So we took the two…it used to go my verse, 'Pac's verse, Money-B's verse. And that was it. Three separate verses. We condensed me and Money-B's verse into one verse and let 'Pac add another verse, and we let 'Pac put it on his album. Smartest thing we ever did. Because it solidified our relationship and image with Tupac…Pac's edge and the fact that…I was talkin' real stuff, not just fantasizing some story about some chick. You know, it was real…Being in the studio with 'Pac made you get serious."

Continuing, Shock G explains that the song was completed in typically-tireless Tupac fashion, such that "what was funny was that after I laid the music to be honest…I was exhausted, and wanted to go home and come back and work on vocals the next day. 'Pac was like, 'No, I gotta get this done now if it's gonna make my album.' I was like, 'Man I don't really have no lyrics yet.' And he was like 'Here,' and he just grabbed a piece of paper, was walking around the studio, and was like, 'Say this.' He gave me at least 70% of what I wound up saying. You know, and I just fixed it to fit me a little bit. But basically, I feel like 'Pac wrote that song. Money-B wrote his own verse. 'Pac wrote most of the rest of it. He told me he wanted some *'Round and round, round we go.'* He didn't have a melody that's all he would say, *'Round and round, round we go.'* I was like, 'OK.' I went into the booth and the music dictated the 'Round and round, round we go.' And I was like, 'Like that?' And I remember 'Pac pressing the button and looking through the glass going, 'Nigga, do you know how good that fuckin' shit sounds!? Yeah, yeah, like that! Keep that! Do it on the next hook to!' Cause everyone in the booth was saying it was start-ing to sound good. I wasn't trippin'…That was his first hit single. His first platinum…gold or platinum selling single. In the end what I am trying to say is that it felt like to 'Pac, to me, to the record company, we all knew Digital had blessed a Tupac record. So far, the biggest things that he had was a 300,000 copy-selling album, if that much. 'Brenda's Got a Baby' did mildly well on the radio. Yeah, he's got a movie coming out. You know, he's doing a movie with Janet (Jackson). But his music thing hasn't been vali-dated yet…So it all felt like we was pluggin' 'Pac. But, as history played itself out it was one of the biggest…it was much more of a help to our career than it was his career. If you take 'I Get Around' out of his thing, he's still got umpteen hits. He's still solidified as an icon. You take 'I Get Around' out of our thing, and it doesn't leave us with much. You know, we've got the Digital hits, but then the association with 'Pac gave us longevity that we wouldn't have had. It gave us street credibility that we wouldn't have had. You know, it gave us a lot of love with 'Pac's fans especially."

Critics were giving Tupac as much love as his fans were by the time of his second album's release, with *Vibe Magazine* hailed 'Strictly for My N.I.G.G.A.Z.' as "an album of extremes—from the frantic shouts of 'Holler If Ya Hear Me' to the glossy sexism of 'I Get Around', to the swingy 'Keep Ya Head Up.' The ferociousness of Tupac's ire and his clearly spoken indignation where the think threads…(bring) the album within a song or two of being a con-cept." The *Source Magazine*, meanwhile, in a 3 1/2 star review, complimented Tupac's sophomore effort as "a combination of '60s black political thought and '90s urban reality, 2Pac is not afraid to speak his mind….balances the gangsta tendencies of street life with insightful revelations." With his newfound critical respect and commercial credibility, Tupac began to carve out his own crew niche with 'Thug Life', a concept Shakur would trans-late into an outright lifestyle and movement in time.

Part II:

Thug Life

1994-1995

Chapter 3
'Thug Life Vol. 1'

The phrase *Thug Life* has become as synonymous with the legacy of Tupac Shakur—by the rap icon's own design—as '*I Have a Dream*' is with Martin Luther King or for that matter, *the Emancipation Proclamation* is with President Abraham Lincoln. All three men died violently as martyrs of the cause of freedom for their African Americans. Each had his own generation of students, representing a different evolution in the state, severity and sophistication of abuses upon the African American community. Each of the aforementioned trio was a diplomat with a different message to deliver, tuned to the times and the adversities that continued to exist, in spite of a Constitutional Amendment tailored to ensure that all people were considered as equal in the eyes of America. Then again, it has long been said that the blindfold on any lady justice statue outside America's courthouses is for her own protection against a systematic abuse of that principle in America's legal system. From Indentured Servitude to Jim Crow voting laws to Rodney King and the L.A. Riots in 1991, by the time Tupac picked up the torch for his black community, the flame of racial shame burned hotter than by-off plots like Affirmative Action or slavery apologies 130 years late could ever hope to appease. Tupac had outright revolution in mind. Groomed for his role as the next link in the chain—the one that would finally break free—from a young age, Shakur's genetic and political roots were those of the Black Panther movement. Employing an equally as militant stance to back up a philosophy for change that could only have been born from a prodigal mind, Tupac's music was a newspaper for the ghetto. Covering the national issues that affected the black community, as well as their every day application upon a people in context of their actions—or reactions—to a system that was irrefutably designed to keep the uprising Tupac had in mind DOWN. As such, he began recruiting through a movement called the Underground Railroad, which he described as "a program…I wanna build all this up, so that by next year you will know the name Underground Railroad…The concept behind this is the same concept behind Harriet Tubman, to get my brothers who might be into drug dealing or whatever it is that's illegal or who are disenfranchised by today's society-I want to get them back into by turning them onto music. It could be R&B, hip-hop or pop, as long as I can get them involved. While I'm doing that, I'm teaching them to find a love for themselves so they can love others and do the same thing we did for them to others." Eventually, the Underground Railroad evolved in time more officially and publicly into Thug Life.

Thug Life Vol. 1, the movement's debut soundtrack, was like a breath of fresh air for hip-hop upon its release in September, 1994. The first legitimate rap GROUP since Public Enemy and N.W.A., the members of Thug Life—Big Syke, Mopreme, The Rated R a.k.a. Ritchie Rich, and Macadoshis—were all seasoned rappers by the time they hooked up with Tupac in late 1993. More like a college football team on their way to the pros than the high school players—who more resembled Shakur's later group, the Outlawz—who displayed the raw talent and promise to succeed in the game, but required years of grooming before they were ready to be hip hop MVPS. Thug Life were veterans of the street game, and most had recorded albums under their belts. A key player on the Thug Life team, and Tupac's best friend, Big Syke elaborates on the latter, explaining that "I met Pac through one of my partners named Surge, and Surge's cousin was actually Pac's manager, (Quatani), at the time. It was just me and Pac hitting me off, and I had an underground album I was doing called Evil Minded Gangstas, and Pac liked the album and what I was doing. It was mainly on some gangsta-type shit, and we hit it off, and he said he wanted to do the 'Thug Life' thing, so I rolled with it. The next thing I know, we're in the studio with a bunch of other cats, and that's when I met Rated, and Macado, and Mo, and Thug Life got poppin'. Later, when I went with Pac over to the Outlawz, not takin' nothing from them, but they was kids. They was the type of cats you put on the front lines as they growin' and as they learnin'. Them other cats from Thug Life, we was already rappin' when Pac met us. The Outlawz was growing, so some was better than others, some you could tell they had been rapping a little longer." Still, for as qualified as the supporting members of Tupac's Thug Life team may have been to play at the level Shakur did, they still all were students to Tupac's coaching in the studio. As Big Syke recalled, "Pac was definitely like our coach in the studio. He was the most inspiring cat I ever been around in my life. So I was like a sponge with him, everything that I could soak up from this cat, I had to. I got ta give alot of credit to Pac, because I was already in the business, but Pac showed me how to take this shit and do it for you, do it the way you want to do it. Put some emotions in your shit. That got me to write some shit like that till I was crying, that was the coldest shit, when you crying and writing some fucking lyrics, they just pouring out you. Pac taught that to the hood, that it was okay to let down that guard."

Thug Life Vol. 1 was a soundtrack for the game, arguably the first, as it had evolved since the epic 'Straight Outta Compton' six years earlier. By 1995, it had become commonplace for a marquee rap act like Tupac to put his posse on following his own initial success—Ice Cube had done it with the Lynch Mob, Ice T with the Rhyme Syndicate, Snoop Dogg with the Dogg Pound, and Biggie Smalls with the Junior Mafia. None of the crews were usually ever as remotely talented as their leader, but because of the street code of a hustler never forgetting his roots, the crew album usually served as a celebration of sorts for the fact that not only had the star rapper made it, but that he had stayed loyal to the block in bringing his boys along. Rappers like Biggie and Ice Cube were usually featured in almost every song on the crew album, typically in the chorus or verse, or sometimes in both if it was a single. Moreover, most crew albums were expected to go gold, selling 500,000 copies as a ceiling. Additionally, most were released within range of the star rapper's initial blow-up in popularity to provide maximum exposure, and capitalize on the lead MC's success in selling his crew. Most industry insiders will acknowledge privately, out of earshot of the superstar MC, that without his support, the crew would never have had a prayer on their own of getting even a development or production deal. Nevertheless, as the trend had become more of a norm, its commonplace had been developed at the promotional level into something of a formula. Typically, the album was driven by a lead single featuring the marquee rapper prominently, usually supported by a video which introduced all the crew members individually flashing money, driving in expensive automobiles, and wearing the requisite diamond-studded label chain of whatever record label they were signed to.

Tupac had something else entirely in mind, moving people rather than moving units, or if nothing else using the album sales as a means toward the end of enlightening his followers to a new way of living life as a hustler. With Thug Life, Shakur was founding a new culture, representative of the realities of the streets, but also the ambitions of a people beyond what Tupac saw as the walls in their own minds based on societal imprisonment via poverty. Tupac sought to lift a people through the Thug Life movement, through a philosophy in which the rapper described as an *Underground Railroad* designed "to get my brothers who might be into drug dealing or whatever it is that's illegal or who are disenfranchised by today's society, I want to get them back by turning them into music. Right now we're twenty strong. The people that are in the UR are coming from all over, Baltimore, Marin City, Oakland, New York, Richmond, all over." Tupac's stepfather Dr. Mutulu Shakur, who Tupac considered his father growing up, explained that "the word 'THUG-LIFE' came from the word Thuggie. The British colonized India and it was a group with in India who resisted the British and they were known as the 'Thuggies'. They had a similar tactic like the Mau Mau's in Kenya. The British used the word Thugs to refer to any group of Outlaws defying oppression. Since Tupac was confronted by exploitation and oppression he accepted the principle and evolved his meaning of it amongst the same lines. We built the code THUG-LIFE to respond to street life here in America." For his part, Big Syke elaborated as a founding member of this movement and as one of its spokesmen on the reasons why Thug Life was appealing to him, as a mirror of most of the movement's recruits on a street level, explaining that "Thug Life was never meant to be a group. It was just the life that we was living. See, when we first started the Thug Life movement, when you said *Thug*, people was like 'Naw, oh no, hell naw.' Pac came with the concept 'Thug Life' originally, and my role was to kinda execute it. I felt I always had to, because always coming in the song after Pac, you better say some shit. Because I knew exactly what he was trying to get to—to make the world understand that whatever the world say is bad, don't mean its bad. Before, everyone was saying *Gangsta,* and I thought I was a gangsta before I met Pac, but then by fuckin' with Pac, I realized I was just a *thug.* It was just the mentality I was brought up around, and it's really the environment that defines the term. Thug life is the nobodies—white, black, brown—any color, and so Thug Life is then just the life we have to life in America, because of the situations we been born into or grew up around, where you ended up in a situation that the world think is bad. The way we dress, the way we talk, it's not right—but in reality, it's just the way we communicate with each other. The world can't tell us how to be."

Not a diamond in the rough, rather a rough diamond, Tupac shined enlightenment in the dawn of the bling-bling age, where Puffy laid waiting to spring those atrocious MC Hammer pants upon us again. The members of Thug Life wore no chains because they were freed through their affiliation to the movement, at least in the sense of being slave to any system—be it that of the dollar to an arrest collar—if Tupac had his way. While most of rap's popular voices surrounding Tupac focused on rapping about how they had escaped the hood, and perhaps had brought a few homies and their immediate family along, Tupac wasn't settling till he took a whole generation with him on the way out. He was more a missionary than a mere diplomat, although he wasn't visiting the hells that he attempted to rescue, he was a native of the struggle of his people. Moreover, in context of white America, the inner city was very much the parallel of an underdeveloped, third-world country systematically oppressed by an economic dictatorship that preferred entitlements to wide-spread employment because it kept the crime rate up, but controlled, and in context of a specific racial demographic. Tupac meant Thug Life to authentically represent the under-dog status of his constituency to its authentic extreme, and he deliberately acted that image out in the eyes of the media to make it stand out as a problem—and he did so successfully. For many who had survived the battlefields of the inner city, they already privately (on in their own neighborhoods) wore their thug status as a badge of honor. Tupac made it fashionable to wear that badge proudly as a lifestyle, as long as responsibilities were taken care of in the process. Tupac didn't want to escape the ghetto till his people did, and as he saw it, they lived vicariously through him in a sense. Big Syke remembers this aspect of Tupac's mentality as one in which "Pac said it best, and it was the hardest shit I ever heard him say, out of all the shit he said, he said 'I might not change the world, but I can bet you I'm gonna spark the brain that will.' If you think about it, that's who Pac was the whole time, he was always taking the covers off of something. Always trying to expose something, the world to the inner city. See, you got to realize he was brung up where if he got in trouble, his mama would make him read the newspaper every day, all the way through. Now, when I was hanging around with him, he used to be reading that newspaper every morning. I didn't know that his upbringing was what made him do that, you feel what I'm saying? He was brung up with this Panther philosophy around him, but yet and still he grew up in the ghetto with the gangstas and the thugs and the hustlers and the pimps, so that's who he was. To me, Pac was an educated nut, he was educated but still going through what all of us went through, from police harassment to being judged by the way he looked, the whole nine. But all his shit was going on TV, and he was really living that shit, it was like rap reality TV man. For instance, when Pac rapped about death—I don't think he wanted to die, but I think when death is around you, by him being so lyrical and open to what he see, that he gonna write down what he see. So when you constantly seeing death around you, and cats trying to kill you—what you think you gonna rap about. You got to rap about what you see and what was going on, and that's one thing he wasn't just good at, he was the best at it. We would see some shit, and by the time we got to that studio, he'd have wrote that shit down and spit it out as soon as we touched down, and I would say to myself, 'Damn! That's shit we just seen.' So he was just like a ghetto reporter, he see it he write it down."

For as wild and controversial as Tupac's life may have played out before the news cameras, in the studio he was all business. Big Syke recalled an environment in which "Pac was the leader, for sure. Every now and then, I'd pull something out, or someone else would pull something out, but most of the time, if it was his session, he was the one to bring it to the table. He always had an idea for something. The order of who went when was usually based off whoever was ready, and it happened to usually be Pac. That's why alot of people wasn't on songs—if you hear those songs on the Thug Life record where Pac doing two verses, it might be him, then it'd be me, then someone else on the back end. But most the time, if the other members didn't show up on the song, its because their verse wasn't ready at the time Pac was working on the song. He never went back to the same song twice, when that session was over, the song was done too. And it could be because you weren't ready, or your verse wasn't tight enough, but Pac was always the judge of that…that was always his call. He'd be like 'Let me hear what it do?' Because he'd write his shit on the spot, then go in that motherfucker, and drop it in one take, and you'd be like 'Woah! Woah shit!' So after him, sometime he wouldn't listen to some of my shit, in particular, but would just say, 'Go on in there if you're ready…' But ready was kind of a loaded word '*ready*', because he'd end that sentence with kind of a warning, 'cause if you ain't ready, don't go up in there.' When I was recording my shit, I had to do whatever it took, because Pac was the teacher. There was alot of things that he brung to the table that I had never seen in the studio. Like going in there, and writing them hooks like it's nothing, and the hook is like the main part of the song. He would go in that motherfucker, and it would be like 'Damn, this sounds like a verse', but then when he do a verse, it sounds like a hook. They were interchangeable, you could do whatever with his shit. He would go in there sometimes and say some shit where I would be like 'Woah, my God.' He would bring the best out of everybody, he made everyone around him good. Cause you know Pac gonna say some shit. And if you following him on a song, you don't wanna even be on the song if your shit ain't coming with something. So that was always to me the philosophy of anyone recording around Pac, it was like—Pac is the best. And no one ever had to tell him. We never had to tell him he was the best, and I don't know if he knew, but we all knew it. I know I knew it, and we never told him, but he never needed to hear it either. He just never said anything, except 'Don't go in there unless you're ready.' He used to say some shit to me, and not just to me, but on song, where you say 'Damn, what made him say that?' Because he used to always say the shit you would only think. That's why he was the best, because he always said the shit you wasn't supposed to be saying, only thinking to yourself, and he would say it. It would just come out his mouth, just as slick as anything, where it come out so natural where it would kind of scare ya. That was his key. I got this saying, 'Pac made crooks read books.'"

Elaborating further on the lessons he took from his studio collaborations with Tupac, Big Syke recalls that "I learned from Pac about writing my lyrics, how to take some words out. If I'm saying too many words here, trying to rush this. He kind of let you do your thing, and just paying attention was just being the best student. Just by watching and seeing how he put songs together would make you a better student, than him having to come over and show you what to do. So I just paid attention to everything from delivery to his lyrical content. If he had a title, then the whole song should be about that title. See, alot of rappers, they just rap. Pac was always staying focused on the subject, so I learned to stay focused on the subject, and no matter what you do, with whatever you say, always make sure you come back and be consistent topically. And he wouldn't really even do it like that all the time, because he could drop a verse, then write a hook, then drop another verse, another verse, then the song done. Me, I would do a hook, then write my verse. Just a different way of doing it, but it all just came out the same. Also, his flows, listen to his shit. Wherever the beat is going, he's throwin' that type of flow on it, he never rapped the same, even though he might have a signature vocal style, his flow was always on some crazy shit, he could switch it up to whatever beat they threw at him. You can hear the cats right now doing them flows of Pac's, you can tell they been studying this nigga, and they not rappin' his words, they rappin' his flows. Look at Jay Z with 'Me and My Girlfriend' for one. That was the whole thing with him in the studio, the flow had to go. It could be your flow, but it better flow on this song. That's what made us work harder. You come after him, so you don't know exactly how he gonna come off on this song, so that makes you say 'Okay, I can't rap on this song like I rapped on the last song. I gotta do something different, I got to flip it up, pause it a little bit—that's why on 'All Eyez on Me', I'm goin' 'So much trouble in the world nigga,' give something a change so the flow would come differently. So it was about the flow and your lyrical content with Pac. Coming in the song after Pac too, you know you better say some shit. If you don't say nothing, the whole song's gonna flop right when you come on, then everybody gonna be waiting for Pac to come back. So the pressure was always on."

Continuing, Syke explains that "another thing I learned from working with Pac was that every beat isn't for you. Just because he could rap over any beat doesn't mean we all got it like that. So when you find a beat that's made for you, that fits you and your style of rap, then you can shine. But if you just rappin' on anything, you would never really be able to shine, because the beat's not really bringing the best out of you. See, so when you was recording with Pac, that was the test of everything—in the process of being with him, you had to learn yourself as an artist. You had to be dissecting yourself as you was working with Pac, because Pac was gonna put your ass on whatever beat. That's why you had to learn how to flow, how to do certain shit that was and wasn't gonna work for your own shit down the line from that experience. Cause listening back, there's certain beats I was on, on some of those albums, that I hated that shit. Cause I didn't like my flow, because I was still learning. It didn't fit me, because I didn't know how to flow on that beat. So in the studio, Pac was always hammering home that that's what its about, learning to flow on that beat to where it sound like you a piece of music on that motherfucker. I learned that from paying attention to him, and then in practice later on my own. I know Pac was the best ever to touch that mic, he could flow on any beat and make it sound like his. His flow was immaculate. In the studio too, Pac was as quick to tell a producer when he didn't like something as he was a rapper. So I learned also to put my foot down, be direct. Pac hated when a producer was in there trying to produce the beat when we was trying to write our lyrics. He didn't like that shit, he'd say 'Lay that fucking beat, let us drop our lyrics, then you can come back later and do all that shit later.' There was an order for sure. I'mma tell you something else about Pac, Pac used to be BANGING on them engineers. If they fucked up, Pac used to go hard on them. I used to feel bad for them motherfuckers. He'd be like 'Why you stop that shit motherfucker. You stop that shit one more mother-fuckin' time, I'mma come up in that motherfucker.' He had a very low tolerance for error. And you gotta think about it, this is before Protools, it was two-inch tape, where the engineer gotta press the button and go all the way back. And Pac don't like to punch, I learned that from Pac too. You don't punch that shit. If you can't drop 16 bars, you might not need to be in there. If there would be some tricky-type flow shit you trying to do, not on his song, if you can't pull it off the first time. He might give you 2 or 3 tries tops to go at it, but that's it. If you fuck up that first time, he's cool, that second time, Pac's gonna be looking at your ass funny. That third time, that shit better be right, and you better be getting ready to do your double. And that double better be perfect, you notice alot of them cats didn't do a double, because they knew better. Because the point of that double, for Pac, was the impact. He definitely set the tone for whatever you gonna try though when you were on his clock. So I learned from him to avoid punching for the most part. I might get to the 14th bar, and fuck up on the last line, so I might have to sneak back in later and fix that. What I would do with Pac was, go in there and drop my shit, then the next day, come in early and do my shit earlier where I knew I'd fucked up. Like 'Imperial, serial killer.' I fucked that up, and DJ Pooh was like 'I'm gonna be in tomorrow, come in tomorrow and fix it.' Because Pac was always like 'Let's go, let's go, let's go, let's go.' So if you fucked up, its gonna be fucked up unless you know the producer, and come in the next day before he get there, and fix your shit. And Pac's point in keeping us on the clock was to teach this: never, never hold up a studio behind getting your lyrics right. Because for the most part, I'd say 98% of the time, Pac never fucked up. He'd get that shit in one take. And when he'd go back and do his layering with tracks, he'd always match his vocals perfectly. And that was before the days when you could edit and line up vocals in Protools. It was unbelievable."

One of Tupac's many talents as a recording artist was his ability to give every song he created its own identity, a process that he passed onto his protégés, including Big Syke, that began with "visualizing the beat in your mind before you rap, as a piece of music—like 'Okay, this is not no regular beat a nigga would be rapping on', and he may be talking topically about the usual shit he talk about, the way he flowed was so different. That's what I'm trying to get into as I get later on in the game, and using another Pac lesson in my music, that every thing I say has to mean something. Cause one day you might be gone, and you have to leave something here for motherfuckers to say 'Damn, that's some real ass shit.' That's what Pac did, he always left that music for you that was timeless like any other great music. That's something else Pac taught me, how to make a song. There's a difference between a song and a rap. See, a song is timeless, where a rap is just where you talkin' bout anything. But its not a song, where you could take the music away and those lyrics actually mean something. You can change the beat on it, like they been doing for years with Pac's shit, update the beats, and the motherfucker still sound like he wrote it yesterday. Pac always said 'Make the music, don't let the music make you.' But he also said 'When you writing some shit, if the music say cry, write some words that make a motherfucker wanna cry. If the music say pull out your guns and start shooting everybody, do that type of song for that type of beat. Whatever the beat tell you, that's what you do. Otherwise, don't fuck with it. If the beat feel happy, make everybody feel happy with the lyrics you write.' That's the bigger picture I learned from Pac, write how the music tell you to write. He always let the words come out as the beat told him to. Also, Pac taught me to stay focused about writing on the pressure and the pain of life, because we had this saying: 'there's more niggas having pain than champagne any day!' Pac always stayed focused on the struggle in his music, so people could always relate to what he rappin' bout. That's what he taught me to stay focused on. Probably one of the most important things Pac taught me in the studio was to make an album full of singles, where you work on every song like that motherfucker could be a single. I remember I had an argument with him in the studio one time, I was like 'Man, let's do some more hard shit.' You know what he told me, 'You want to cater to these niggaz in the hood, or you wanna sell records?' I feel like from that conversation, I learned how to make a smoother song over time, shit like that is an everlasting point on your life when you come from that street background. It's hard to change as a person, but harder as an artist—to grow out of that mentality. He made me believe I could give them cats something back that would inspire they lives and change a motherfucker. And his secret in that was to make them all singles. Cause Pac, for all his big songs, they was either 'bout sex/partying like 'I Get Around', 'How Do You Want It,' about women, or some serious thinking-ass songs, the ones that make you wanna cry, 'Keep Ya Head Up', 'Dear Mama', 'Brenda's Got a Baby.' Them three situations was the subject of the biggest songs of all time in hip hop, the platinum hits had those three common denominators. Those kinds all consist together as far as Pac was concerned. It was fucked up too, because when Pac was recording, he never knew which were gonna be the singles. We just did songs, but he was so talented, every song he bang out could have been a single. He just treated every song he did like it could have been a single, which raised his expectations for everyone working around him too."

Tupac and Big Syke began their collaboration together during the making of Thug Life Vol. 1, which it may surprise fans to know, according to the latter crew member, when recording began "there were two Thug Life albums. The first Thug Life album that got made never came out, so the one that eventually came out wasn't even the original album. So alot of the songs that ended up on that album got done later, after they decided they was gonna make us a group. Interscope made us like a group, but the first Thug Life album had Ritchie Rich, Warren G, Nate Dogg, all kinda cats on it. But they watered it down to make it like a group. So it ended up being me, Rated R, Mopreme, Macadocious, and Pac." As the official Thug Life Vol. 1 album took shape, one of the key topics on the minds of all the group's members was the loss of friend Big Kato, who Tupac, along with his fellow group members, frequently shouted out on songs throughout the album. One song in particular that authentically captured the group's pain was 'How Long Will They Mourn Me', which Big Syke recalled was inspired by "my homeboy, Big Kato. Alot of people don't know that, but that was my partner, I grew up with that cat. And I hooked him up, and we hung out with Pac, and Pac took to him, and the hung out one night, went to a club when we was in Atlanta. So after that, Pac really loved Big Kato. We all put it down on that album for Kato." In addition to the long-term collaboration between Tupac and Big Syke that originated out of Thug Life, Shakur also met producer Johnny J during the making of this album, not surprisingly through Big Syke. Recalling the circumstances that led to their meeting, Johnny J recalls that "the way Pac and I hooked up was, basically, a situation where how we met was, I was working with another artist from Thug Life, Big Syke—I was producing his album, an underground joint called 'Evil Minded Gangstas.' When we met, it was a thing where I already had some of the music done and ready to go, when we started out with 'Pour Out a Little Liquor' back in the days of Thug Life, which also went on the soundtrack to 'Above The Rim.' I already had most of that music preset and ready to go." Elaborating on the process of producing his first songs with Tupac, Johnny remembers that "I ended up sharing my beats with both of them on Thug Life Volume 1, which was our first collaboration, mine and Pac's. It was a beautiful thing. After that, we did 'Death Around the Corner' on 'Me Against the World.' Originally, that track had been a part of the Thug Life sessions, and Pac and I had cut like 10 songs in a 3-day period, which kind of became our M.O. after he got out of prison, working around the clock like that. On the first day I met him, we did 'Pour Out a Little Liquor', and in that same first day, another track called 'Thug Life', and 'Death Around the Corner.' Then 'Ready for Whatever', 'Fake Ass Bitches', we were just knocking shit out."

Another producer who worked on the Thug Life album, Warren G, recalls his collaboration with Tupac as one in which "2Pac was incredible man, he was down to earth, real, and just an incredible worker! He was a hard worker. When I wasn't nothin', I was NOTHING back in the days, I was trying to get put on. This dude calls me at 10 o'clock at night, I'm layin' on the floor at my sisters house, no money, glasses on with tape on the side, I got a needle trying to hold on a arm, I'm in a house on the floor. He calls me 10 o'clock at night, tells me, 'Warren I need a beat!' Cause he heard how I did Indo Smoke, so he knew I could do tight ass beats...Tupac said 'Warren you got a beat?' We did 'How Long Will They Mourn Me.' And I told 2Pac, 'You know what? Nate Dogg would sound TIGHT on this motherfucker.' So I called Nate, and told him 2Pac wants him to come and do this hook. Nate came over there and layed that bitch down. Hit record! And that was like some of my first studio experiences...I think this soundtrack me and Tupac did with John Singleton really launched my career." Thug Life was completed in the summer of 1994, at the same time Tupac was beginning work on what would become his third solo album, 'Me Against the World.' Ever-present at these sessions, Shakur-sidekick Big Syke remembers that "'Me Against the World' was going on the same time that Thug Life was going down. If you remember, the album that came out right before he came to jail was Thug Life, then when he went to jail, 'Me Against the World' came out." Released on September 20, 1994, 'Thug Life Vol. 1' quickly went Gold, and received positive reviews as a soundscape for Tupac's evolving movement, with *Vibe Magazine* commenting that the record was "compelling...the groove hits the spot…N.W.A.'s 'Straight Outta Compton' came out as strong and progressive as…Thug Life Volume 1" *Entertainment Weekly*, for its part, raved that "you've got to hand it to Tupac… (Thug Life Volume One) crackles with kinetic energy…ONE proves that more isn't necessarily merrier, but it's definitely more thrilling." While the fall of 1994 would prove to be the most tumultuous of Tupac's career outside the studio to date, inside the lab he stayed typically busy working away on 'Me Against the World.'

Chapter 4
'Me Against the World'

Released on February 27th, 1995, 'Me Against the World' became Tupac Shakur's first number one album, quickly going double-platinum, and producing the hits 'Temptations' and 'Me Against the World', as well as the smash gold single and Grammy-nominated 'Dear Mama.' Arguably the first rapper to defy hip-hop's undeniable obsession with chauvinistic lyrics and speak outright in celebration and defense of the black female struggle, 'Dear Mama' was an evolution from the days of 'Brenda's Got a Baby' and 'Keep Ya Head Up.' A much more personal ode to the millions of single, black mothers who had raised his genera-tion of young, black males, the song became an instant anthem for millions upon millions of young, black **females**. As perhaps the only rapper with the artistic ability and hood credibility to speak on behalf of both African American men and women in the same time and song, Tupac made his greatest statement for any women's rights movement existent within broader hip hop culture to date with 'Dear Mama.' Written as a thank-you letter to his mother, Afeni Shakur, producer Tony Pizarro, describing the making of 'Dear Mama', recalled that the song was inspired out of the fact that "Pac used to make reference to 'Dear Mama' in a lot of differ-ent songs and I'd always comment like 'You know that's a song in itself.' And one day he was like 'I got something for that.' And he was like 'Man, you have *In my Wildest Dreams* by the Crusaders and I was like 'Yeah.' He was like 'Yeah, I got something for that.' So I got the track ready. Pac just came through and just dropped it and blessed it with them vocals…And for me, that's pretty much been the story of my life too. I kind of really knew what do to as far as putting that hook together because at that particular time, that was my story. I hadn't really talked to my mom for a while. So my whole thing was like putting that hook together, making sure that it was letting mom's know that you were appreciated."

As singular as the experience of recording 'Dear Mama' may have been, Pizarro's overall experience in the studio with Tupac was common in one respect, that being his job requirement as a producer to keep up with Shakur's rapid-writing and recording pace, such that "Pac could write them lyrics right there on the spot, like basically behind the mic…I remember Tupac specifically at one point, he'd write the lyrics in probably less than 5 minutes, write a verse and be like 'Tone I'm a go in the booth now.' After he would record the first verse he would be like, 'Alright play that back. This is what you gon do. You gon play it back one time and the second time when you play it back just punch me and record.' And when I would press record there would be the lyrics to the rest of the song and those particular lyrics wouldn't even be written, and the song would be done, boom rap. And that could be like 20 minutes. Pac could record like 6 songs in a night, finished, lyrics, hooks, everything. Being around Pac, it was very obvious and very evident. Here was a man who finally reached his goal and what he had set out to do and now that he actually made it."

The producer who worked perhaps most elaborately with Tupac on the making of 'Me Against the World' was Easy Mo Bee, who recalled the collaboration as a learning experience, wherein "Tupac… had a particular recording process, and that is like—when (he) started recording, (he) didn't want you to stop, and (he) didn't like to do punch-ins. In other words, a songtypically has three verses. And Tupac…would have you start the tape and let it run all the way through the song. 'Don't stop. Don't punch me,' in other words. Some people do a verse and stop, and do a second. (Pac) did not like to stop…he nailed in one take. If there's anything I got from him in those sessions, it's you don't have to be perfect. Just be yourself and put all of your heart and soul into it... (Tupac), in the studio between sessions...he would just spit, what I would call, reality raps. The average East Coast rapper, when he freestyles, he's freestyling some braggadocios, material, this and that. But Tupac, it amazed me, he had the ability to freestyle reality type raps. He'd talk about what's going on in the world, police brutality, whatever." One of the hits from the album the duo collaborated on as 'Temptations', in which Mo Bee recalled that "I went on the set of 'Above the Rim.' I visited him while he was in New York at the Ruckers Grounds. During one of his breaks in the film, what he did was—he went in the trailer and I played him some music. He was like, 'That's cool and everything,' he picked a couple of them, but then he asked me, "Could you do something for me with 'Computer Love' And the 'Computer Love' one became 'Temptations.' When he asked me to do (it), I said, 'So many people have (sampled this) before, what am I gonna do different?' Throw it on 45, speed it up, filter it so you muffle it, getting nothing but the bass frequencies out of it, and then I went around that —built new drums, new keyboards, later I got the idea to add the Erick Sermon 'Heyyy' from Redman's album. That's how I got 'Temptations.'...Lyrically, he's talking about a relationship with a female. He's saying basically, 'I like the time I'm spendin' with ya, but baby, I'm busy." He has intonations he has in there remind of a record that Bobby Womack did called 'You'll Be There When the Sun Goes Down.' They talked about the same thing. 'Don't get hung up on me.' (And Pac had) mentioned to me, kind of what he wanted to talk about. Then, in the end, after he wrote it, 'cuz he would write with a pen and a pad. He was like, 'Check this out,' went in the booth, and it all worked out."

Vibe Magazine's review of 'Me Against the World' hailed Shakur's third album as his realest, such that "Tupac lets go of his usual theme of thuggery-as-resistance...He ponders, on 'If I die 2Nite', whether 'heaven got a ghetto for thug niggaz.' By the final verse, he's hoarse, spitting words out like they taste bitter: 'Don't shed a tear for me, nigga/I ain't happy here.' It's an ice-cold song, way beyond words. But amid all his righteous venom, Pac, as is his practice, dispenses maxims. 'Always do your best,' he says over bouncy music of the title song…He draws you in with these little do-good moments—he seems, like this album, to schizo enough to be interesting, just crazy enough to be sincere…Tupac can make hope sound as real as all the fucked-up shit. He proved it last time out—coming out of his mouth, the idea of keeping your head up doesn't sound corny at all." *Rolling Stone Magazine*, for its part, commented in a 3 1/2 star review that the album was "by and large a work of pain, anger and burning desperation—is the first time 2Pac has taken the conflicting forces tugging at his psyche head-on." *The Source Magazine* gave the album a coveted 4 stars and raved that the record was "his best work by far…a manifestation of Tupac's talents becoming completely whole." *All Music Guide*, meanwhile, in its 5-star review identified the album as "the point where 2Pac really became a legendary figure.

Having stared death in the face and survived, he was a changed man on record, displaying a new confessional bent and a consistent emotional depth…This is 2Pac the soul-baring *artist*, the foundation of the immense respect he commanded in the hip-hop community. It's his most thematically consistent, least-self-contradicting work, full of genuine reflection about how he's gotten where he is—and dread of the consequences…These tracks—most notably 'So Many Tears,' 'Lord Knows,' and 'Death Around the Corner'—are all the more powerful in hindsight with the chilling knowledge that he was right…Overall, Me Against the World paints a bleak, nihilistic picture, but there's such an honest, self-revealing quality to it that it can't help conveying a certain hope simply through its humanity. It's the best place to go to understand why 2Pac is so revered; it may not be his definitive album, but it just might be his best." Industry-wide, it was agreed, against the backdrop of Tupac's constantly controversial life, life imitated art on 'Me Against the World.'

Artistically, Shakur had finally bottled his lightning, such that, as one of the rapper's friends and producers DJ Quik saw it, on 'Me Against the World' "after he had some experiences in his life and some people turned on him, and I've actually seen some people who actually did him bad and turned on him and they can talk about it with such pride that these days it just makes me sick. And that whole energy, you know, it was a lot on him so he became more cathartic when he did Me Against The World and he let that shit out and I'm glad he did because that was when he started to shine his light." Echoing Quik's sentiment, Tupac himself claimed 'Me Against the World' as "my truth. (Its) my best album yet... When you do rap albums, you got to train yourself. You got to constantly be in character. You used to see rappers talking all that hard shit, and then you see them in suits and shit at the American Music Awards. I didn't want to be that type of nigga. I wanted to keep it real...I'm not a gangsta rapper. I rap about things that happen to me. I got shot 5 times, you know what I'm saying? People was trying to kill me. It was really real like that. I don't see myself being special; I just see myself having more responsibilities than the next man. People look to me to do things for them, to have answers...(On this album), I laid it down, (so) I can be free."

Chapter 5
The Outlawz

Tupac conceived the Outlawz while in sitting in Clinton Correctional Facility, plotting his next move in what would become Hip Hop's biggest and arguably most hostile take-over in context of the East Coast/West Coast beef. Without regurgitating the widely-popularized specifics of the coastal dispute, it was clear heading into the storm that Tupac seemed to feel as though he wanted his a tight circle of allies to watch his back, so he recruited Big Syke and Mo'Preme from Thug Life, family members, and members of an Atlanta clique called Dramacydal to form the Outlaw Immortalz. What was fascinating about the Outlawz—more in context of the sum necessarily than the individual members—was the concept that inspired the group, rooting from a philosophical and historical depth and sophistication that Hip Hop had not witnessed prior to Tupac. Its every rapper's dream to snatch a notorious pseudonym as their alter ego or professional namesake—be it Scarface, Frank White, Gotti, and so forth—but no one saw a 15th Century philosopher studied by virtually every great leader of the past 5 millenniums coming. By taking the alias Niccolo Machiavelli—perhaps history's greatest political strategist, wrote the bibles on modern political philosophy and military strategy respectively, The Prince and The Art of War—Tupac was innovating even the teachings of this great philosopher, as Shakur was both feared and loved equally. Most leaders settled for one or the other. While the core members of the group had been featured on the track 'Outlaw' from Shakur's 'Me Against the World' album, the group was still evolving as a concept when Tupac's career was interrupted with his prison sentence. As Tupac himself described the philosophy behind the Outlawz concept, "I got a kids group that deals with the problems a younger generation is going through. They put them into rhymes so it's like a psychology session set to music."

Outlawz member Big Syke remembers the circumstances surrounding the inception of the group's name and concept, recalling that "Pac was sitting in Clinton, and he came out into the visitors area, and sat down with us and gave us our names. Cause we were sitting up talking about what the names gonna be, and I came up with 'Boss Playa' for myself, and Pac was like 'Naaah,' and he kept shooting down everybody's little nick names they had given themselves. Then we came back the next day to see him again, and he was like 'We gonna be the 'Outlaw Immortalz.' And I didn't really know what immortal meant at the time, and Pac was always saying some words that made a motherfucka get the dictionary out. From there, the individual names he gave us, all these guys was dictators, powerful leaders. They all led some motherfuckers to the point where, for us to be able to say they names, they immortalized themselves. So as far as rappers, as long as we fuckin' with Pac, we immortalized as well, because as long as they talk about Pac, sooner or later they gonna have to do stories on some of these other motherfuckers."

"That was his strategy. Pac immortalized himself, as we can all see, so now that's what we got to do. Not only us, but anybody who's trying to make a change in the world. It was about legacy as a group, but also individually, if you look at these names, these leaders—whether good or bad—made a statement on the world, made a dent on the world. It ain't just about music, for Pac it was larger than that, it was about being immortalized when your ass is up out of here. When he named his shit Makaveli, he named me Mussolini, then there was Komani, who was Mo'Preme, Pac's half-brother, Kastro, his boy Napolian, Hussein Fatal, who was Pac's cousin,

Kadafi—who was a close friend of Tupac's from childhood, and whose mother had been involved with Afeni Shakur in the Black Panther movement years earlier, and E.D.I. Mean—he named everybody. He gave everybody they names. I didn't know who the fuck Mussolini was, but I had to go read up on this cat, Pac made me go read. I had to go hit the books to find out this cat was a dictator from back in the day from Italy, and hung out with Hitler, and his momma and his daddy were teachers in the little political thing, trying to get some shit going. But I had to read that, and Pac knew who that cat was when he gave it to me, but that's why I had to read up on it—to see why he named me this cat. Even with Makiavelli, and Napolian, and Mussolini,, all them cats was leaders of they time. So what they did, they was people who could move the masses, and that's what I got in terms of the bigger picture off of Pac. No one else could have thought up that shit but him. Did you listen to some of the shit Pac did on that Makiavelli album, that didn't sound like no Tupac album. It was Pac, but it was an artistic evolution, because the words coming out his mouth was so cold, that you always gonna have somebody sayin' they seen Pac, cause Makiavelli faked his death. He's like the black Elvis. Pac was always constantly reinventing himself. That's the path he tried to get us to follow as members of the Outlawz."

Outlawz member Napolian, who Tupac often referred to as his protégé, remembers being put on by Shakur into the Outlawz clique as a life-transforming event that saved him from a violent upbringing that had begin with his witnessing his parent's murder at age 3. Recalling that "the first time I recorded with Pac, I was 16 years old. The first time I met the brother, I moved to Atlanta, and I was in a group called Young Thugz, which became Dramacydal— and had Kadafi, E.D.I., Kastro, and then me. One of the first songs he ever put me on was 'Me Against the World.' I was a teenager at the time, and wasn't living the life of a normal teenager, but when I got around Pac, I had to grow up. He wanted us to grow up, stay focused, and because he put his heart and soul into the music. Half of the Outlawz is his family members. So I remember Pac used to go around to people saying 'This is cousin Edi, my cousin Kastro, my brother Kadafi, this is my homeboy Fatal, he's the lieutenant, this is my homeboy Mousilinni, homeboy Noble, and this is my protégé Napolian. So I used to think 'Why the hell he keep calling me his protégé?' I guess he seen something in me that I didn't see at the time, when I was around him, I didn't always feel like I had it in me, but I guess Pac knew I had it in me more than I did. So when he was around, it was always 'I got to step it up, I gotta step it up. I guess Pac got some hope in me, and I can't be lazy, so let me not make fool out of him. He believe in me, so let me believe in myself and step my game up."

Tupac's artistic confidence building process was a tough course that he ran with the discipline of a Texas high school football coach, keeping his players on a steady diet that, as Outlawz member Napolian recounted, involved constant recording, constructive criticism, patience, respect, tough love, and good times amid all of the aforementioned. As Napolian recalled the specifics of Tupac's regimen, "Pac ran a tight ship during the recording sessions. One thing I can say about the dude is he was serious about what he do. He loved his art, his acting—but when he gets into the studio, he becomes a whole other person—he becomes a genius. And what we learned from the guy is you have to always stay focused. Pac was definitely one of them guys who wanted you to stay focused. So we was kind of like students in Pac's class. He was a very disciplined type of dude, and we lived with him, so we was around him all the time. So there would be days where we would be going from the studio straight to a movie set, and we'd be tired, but if go to sleep, he'd be ready to fine us, or threaten to send us back home. He had us on military type tactics. He definitely was a special individual, because we was all kids back then, and we all make mistakes as humans, but we made HUNDREDS of mistakes, and I always wondered what gave him the patience to stick around with us. He stuck with us, he was a good teacher.

From working with him, it gave me confidence as an artist, and made me feel like I could do better, and that's the way Pac was, he always knew we could get better too. In terms of my recording process, things I take directly from my working with Pac is, for one, every time I do a song, I double my vocals. Another thing I took from Pac was to talk about the true stuff, and the pain that people go through—the real life. None of that bling-bling shit, even when I am positive, I am still real. Another thing I learned from the brother—when you do music, you pretend the beat is your diary, and whatever come out your heart, you put it on the paper, and then the record. He also always taught us not to care what people think about it. One other thing Pac taught me was never, ever be scared to say what you want to say. Talk about the stuff that's really happening in the world, not the popular trends, and in time, your shit will become what's popular because so many people will relate to it."

Elaborating more specifically on Tupac's recording process with the group, Napolian explained that "how he usually do it was, he'd hear one of Johnny's beats, and go 'We doin' that beat. You doin' 8, you doin' 8', and he'd tell us all to write 8 bars. He'd go in there, write his shit in 5, 10 minutes, boom , spit it out. Come out, 'Who ready? Whoever ready, Go. If you ain't ready, I'mma do the other.' If the other two verses weren't ready, he'd say 'The hell with y'all, I'mma get back on the song.' He worked like that, so it was never really where he was approving our verses ahead of time, like 'Change this, I don't like that.' He never really was that type of guy. You just didn't want to follow him and be wack, so we was all trying to put our best down. We lived with him and we was so comfortable with him because we was around him 24-7. So we'd pull up to the sessions with him, and leave with the studio with him. When Pac had a beat sometimes, he'd let us hear it at his house, and we'd write to it before we went in to record. But one thing about Pac, he'd always say 'Y'all better have your verses finished when I go in to lay mine.' One thing about the dude, the

Man did so many songs. And he wasn't afraid to bounce anybody, if you was wack, you was coming off the song. It wasn't nothing personal, it was business, but Pac did it with such a good heart, so he never tried to embarrass anybody. You just come in one day and might not hear your vocals there. He showed everybody respect. The ones who don't show respect are the ones who aren't from the street—they the ones who hurt people's feelings, say 'Get the hell out of there.' They don't know who's in the streets, and the rule there is always you don't disrespect anybody till they disrespect you. So one thing about Pac, he respected everybody. I'll look back now and listen to some of the songs I did with Pac, and be like 'What the hell was I talking about? That was wack.' But Pac was such a real dude, that he just let us do what we wanna do, as long as we could pull it off in a take or two at the most. Most of the time, Pac was so fresh that whatever come out, he just keep it. So he applied that approach to us too. He used to say 'Whatever you lay, we keepin' it, go on to the next song. We don't have time to play, we don't have time to be on the song for 30 minutes.' He was that type of brother. He had a good heart, he always thought about other people's feelings. Pac was also one of those type of dudes though, that if he did take you off the track, you kept your mouth shut about it and just do better next time, because if you say something he don't like and cross him, you got it coming. So don't take his kindness for granted."

The street code that Tupac and the Outlawz brought off the block and into the studio, as Napolian reasoned, was a job requirement "because it was Death Row, so there was always street people around us, so you don't know who you dissin'. Its like a whole other code of ethics, but we just kept it the same in the studio too. But one thing about Pac, when it was time to go up in the studio, he never let us bring no groupies with us, he was a smart man. He don't play that groupie thing, but all his homeboys was there, alot of the Death Row artists. When Suge was around too, it was all love, they crack jokes all day. But even Suge never got in the way of

Pac working, he let Pac perform the way he perform. Cause couldn't no one keep up with us over there. He kept it very disciplined in the studio, and Suge had to appreciate that. Most of the recording we did with Pac was with Johnny J, especially in the Death Row days, Johnny was his main dude. Aside from the Makaveli album, Johnny J did everything. Their chemistry was nice—and the sessions was always cool, we crack jokes alot, and was always smokin', drinkin', but Pac and Johnny always kept working through that. It wasn't like you go to your job and you're scared to smile cause you might get fired though. They kept it professional, but we was still allowed to be kids. Work oriented, but we also got to have a good time."

An essential anchor to keeping the recording sessions moving at the same pace they would absent the Outlawz, producer Johnny J explained that he and Tupac treated the sessions much like a training camp for hip hop's newest recruits, wherein "they were still in their learning stages, still learning how to write fast, and stay on point with delivering vocals, because Pac would give them a time frame: 'If you don't have this done in 30 minutes, or by the time I'm done writing my verse, you're not on the record.' So it was literally like a writing Olympics. Like a fucking contest. He was definitely like a coach with them, but he wasn't only hard on them, he would take alot of different tracks depending on the situation. Sometimes when the Outlawz were recording, they would have issues with doubling their vocals, or getting it on time, or they'd stumble on words. He was a hell of a coach to those guys, Pac would say things like 'You guys gotta pick up your game, elevate your levels dude. Because if you don't, this shit is definitely not going down.' We stayed on it together. They were good on the bars, but on overall vocal delivery—they would stumble sometimes, run out of breath. There would be breathing issues, trying to get so many words out in one breath, which you can't do. They see Pac get it all out, and think 'Oh shit, I can go in there and do the same thing.' It was almost like he was a motivator for him, but they would stumble. And if there was liquor around the session, that could cause problems for some of them, because they were young, they were kidz growing up. Trying to hang with the big boys, so we taught them sometimes you got to bow down, and learn first."

Despite the training camp Tupac was running with the Outlawz in the studio, according to member Big Syke a.k.a. Mussolini, while the group was certainly an the opportunity of a lifetime for each member, it was in no way charity case, such that "one thing I can say about every cat that Pac had in the Outlawz and Thug Life, every one of us could rap. Every rapper had his own shit, if you took a best song from each of us, all of us could have a hit." While many of the members of the Outlawz were minors, and certainly green to the game even if they were of-age, veterans like Mo'Preme and specifically Big Syke, saw themselves as big brothers to Tupac's father-figure role in the group's dichotomy, such that, as Syke defined it, "my role within the Outlawz was like Pac's Lieutenant, but I just looked at it was—I need to stay ground level, and that it stayed street around there. That's what I felt my job was, because I was from the street, and everything that we was rappin' about, I basically done did or tried. So I always felt I was the certification of everything we was rapping about, and I felt it was also my job to help the next cats with whatever—the game, whatever they might need to know, I'm gonna tell you whether you want to hear it or not. Pac and me both always was tryin' to teach the Outlawz, or any other younger cats we had around. I always felt like them cats was like my little brothers. So you don't want them to go and do something stupid, you want them to try and uphold something you represent."

Elaborating on what he and Tupac were trying to teach the group as a sampling of the larger generation they were trying to reach through the Thug Life/Outlawz movement, Syke explained that "Pac and I was always telling them 'Don't none of you all ever bring this Outlaw and Thuglife thing down. You can never put no tarnish on this shit.' So we tried to teach them the Game—which we saw as life, the game of life. The game is really filling the gaps that these other cats talk about, who glorify the life—which I do sometimes too—that its not just about bustin' a cap, but telling 'em why you pullin' the trigger too. See, they need to have a class called consequences, cause they teach you all kinda shit in school, but they don't teach you about life. And its the game of life: knowing to see problems before they occur, knowing that this motherfucker liable to try and get you before he help you. The game is what you learn in the street that you can spread to somebody else that they don't know. Die with some loyalty, die with some honor. Don't be no snitch, just worry about you. Try to do the best that you can do, and don't hate on nobody else for doing what they doing. Which sometimes is a thin line, because if you don't like somebody, you sort of turn into a hater. So we always contradicted ourselves with some of the shit that we did, but that's life, and life is contradicting, and Pac was really the first rapper to speak on that for us as a community. The Lawz was like a little sample of that community he was speaking to."

Upon his exit from Prison in (March), 1995, Big Syke remembers that not much had changed about Tupac's personality, other than his priorities had been clarified—those being taking care of business in the studio, and his family and friends in the process, such that "Pac loved his niggaz, I don't think Pac liked being alone. I ain't never seen him alone. We kept in touch when he was in jail, I never talked to him on the phone, but I damn sure saw him in person through visits. The last month he was inside before he got out, I was up there. I stayed at a hotel like 20 minutes away from there, waiting on him to get out. The date kept getting moved, so we just stayed there till he got out. I don't think much changed from before he went in to when he got out, Pac is Pac man. He—even though he went to jail and all that—when he got out, was about the same shit, it was just him. Jail didn't change his work ethic as far as I was concerned, because he was always doing the same thing—working. That's why he got so many mother-fuckin' songs, cause he was always working. He didn't just start working when he got out the jailhouse, he was working before he went in there. He had 50, 60 unreleased songs that hadn't come out before he went into jail. So then, when he came out, he got 100 or more songs, and there you go. Pac was the type of cat who—if you got a beat—and he like it, he gonna fuck with it. So some of that shit that never came out, it was the situation where Pac being Pac, he would have gotten on any motherfuckin' beat and ride that motherfucker. So most of the beats he got on, he was better than the beat. It was like the beats couldn't handle him." Outlawz member Napolian, who was with Tupac from the day of his release onward on almost a constant basis, for his part noticed a definite change in Tupac upon his exit from prison that he described as "extra fire in him. When he came home from jail, he went wild in the studio. Before he went into prison, he was more laid back, but when he came out, he was definitely more serious. He was on a whole other level, it seem like." With the Outlawz in tow, Tupac headed out to California to begin what would become the most artistically prolific and commercially high-profile period of his life, and most glorious in that of larger hip hop's.

Part III:
The Death Row Days

1995-1996

Chapter 6
Lightning in a Bottle-Tupac and Johnny J

Hip Hop has given us some truly inspired producer/rapper fellowships over the years—Erik B. and Rakim, Dr. Dre and well... everybody from Snoop Dogg, Eminem, D.O.C., and Ice Cube; and some might say Biggie and P. Diddy. For the late Tupac Shakur, no one more naturally assumed that title than Johnny J—and together, they completed the ring, bringing rap full circle in its first revolution. The course by which emcees and their producers come to work together is often random. In other cases, it seems fated, if in Tupac and Johnny J's instance, by no other illustration than the 150+ musical masterpieces they composed together in the last 8 months of Shakur's life. Johnny J, for his part, felt what would become his collaboration with Tupac was a matter of euphonious destiny, such that "prior to Pac and I meeting, I was doing alot of instrumentals, but didn't have vocals that were meeting the ability of where my music was going. It was sad, I felt like I was doing instrumentals just to do beats, just entertaining myself, just to listen to my own music. But there were no lyrics or type of written concepts which matched what I was doing—until I met Tupac. Then I knew—this is where it all begins. I felt it was kindred, like we were definitely meant to collaborate together. Without a doubt, it felt so good. It's hard to explain, but I know the chemistry was meant to be, it was written. When the lyrics first touched down on my tracks, I felt like I was in heaven, I felt like 'Oh my God, what a relief.' And I wasn't even looking at the fact that he was Tupac, I wasn't on this star-struck type of shit, I was just like 'Finally, an artist who knows what the fuck to do to my beats.' And he looked at me like 'Finally, a producer who knows how to bring music to my lyrics.' It was that look in his eye, like 'I found what I needed.' " Big Syke, who introduced Tupac and Johnny J, recalled that "it was a great fit, Tupac and Johnny J working together, because Johnny was just like Pac: he was always at the studio making beats, and he was there at the perfect time to make that perfect combination, because Dre wasn't there, and Johnny was the one who could keep pullin' up them beats. And Pac dug his beats consistently, so as long as he kept pullin' up them beats, Pac gonna keep rappin'."

Elaborating for his part, Johnny J explains that "I met Pac through my work with Big Syke on 'Evil Minded Gangstas.' So word got around, and when Pac heard the beats I had done on Syke's album, he said 'You gotta introduce me to the dude who did your beats.' And Syke was like 'No problem, that ain't but a phone call away.' Next thing I know, I get a call, 'Tupac wants to meet you, I'mma come pick you up, why don't you bring some beats.' So it started right there, that plain and simple. I didn't have to shoot any demos, didn't have to prove shit, he heard my shit on Syke's record, and was like 'I need who did your beats on my shit.' So it was funny, they had the funniest chemistry over the whole thing, because Syke was like 'Hey, that's my producer!' Then Tupac was like 'Naw, that's my producer!' They had fun about it." Thug Life Vol. 1 allowed Johnny and Tupac the opportunity to transition their collaboration from Tupac's group project to Shakur's solo realm, where the two felt much more at home. At the time, Tupac was in the process of completing work on 'Me Against the World', his third album, which would become his most successful to date, allowing Tupac to expand commercially, and providing Johnny in the same time with the chance to—within that expansion—begin to rewrite what the producer felt was a trend toward "overcrowding in hip hop production at the time, where there was a little too much going on in the music. I didn't like that there were too many overdubs, too much going on in the drum aspect of things. So when 'Death Around the Corner' ended up on 'Me Against the World' I felt like that was a good transition for me, because the first hit song I'd ever produced was Candy Man's 'Knockin' Boots', that whole album I did right out of high school in 1991, for Epic Records. And that was the more mellow 'I Need Love' type of shit, that kind of rap. The mellow, pretty stuff, what the ladies like. So it felt good to transition from that over to the type of beats I was doing with Tupac, where I got to show 'Here's some aggressive shit', where I could still lay pretty music, but Pac brought alot more aggression to it, alot more realism to the shit. So from that time when I first started working with Pac until now, when I've been producing, I've never changed my formula even to this day, I kept it pretty simple. But I knew during that time period, when we first met, break records were in at the time, so we were using alot of breaks, but I was still putting my original drum track to it. But I noticed that most of the shit that I would do around it was sounding better than using the break beats, so after I took the break record off of my beat, I thought that this was really more the shit I need to do—keep the production simple and too the point. Which also allowed his words more room to breathe on the track."

Sadly, shortly after the magic had started to kindle, Johnny and Tupac's creative flame would be temporarily blown out by the 11 month incarceration Shakur was sentenced to as a result of his sexual assault conviction in late 1994. Johnny, for his part, felt that Shakur's imprisonment was the creative equivalent of snatching a new born baby from his mother's arms, in context of the musical evolution the two were developing together. From the jump, as Johnny saw it, "the music I made with Tupac elevated the potential for where his artistic ability could go. I really felt that I was the motivational piece that he needed, the missing link. I

51

know I was the missing link that he needed to take his concepts and his vocal styles to another level. And I've been complimented for that, people say to me all the time, 'Johnny, when Pac met you, it definitely elevated him to another level that he needed.' Because there was a time period—proceeding his incarceration—where he was kind of limited, where he didn't really take it as far as he really should have, or really wanted to because the music wasn't meeting him there. It wasn't hitting where he needed it, and I was the one who brought it to the table, and that's where it all went to the next level. Once we'd discovered that connection—unfortunately—not too long after that, Tupac went to jail, and it felt like the world ended on me. That's where it felt like walls collapsed. And I was asking 'Why did this have to happen? Why did the chemistry have to stop because of some shit like that?' So when he was inside, that was kind of like a hiatus for me, because I did wait for him. I felt as though the walls had caved in, like 'What happened?' It was like my other musical half had left, he was no longer here. I can't have him in the studio. It put me into a slump, into like a deep depression, because I was like 'Oh, I'm back to doing instrumentals again.' Because wasn't nobody else going to rap on my shit while he was inside. And there was a period during those 9 months where I stopped doing music, I stopped creating. I said 'I don't wanna do any music right now, I wanna give it a break.' Because I felt as though, without him being there with me at that level, why should I continue doing beats when I don't have the lyrics I need on it?"

In a musical sense, it seemed the two men were definitely serving their time together. Still, perhaps in an effort to rally Tupac's artistic cause on the outside, or alternately because the music started playing so loudly in Johnny's head that he had to let it pour out of him and onto tape—usually a musician's only means to turn that volume down—he started writing again in anticipation of Shakur's release. As Johnny tells it, "after a while, I just went back to work, and just started creating beat after beat after track after track waiting for him to get out, and it ended up becoming some of the songs you hear on 'All Eyes on Me.' Some of those songs were created while Pac was in jail, so they were almost fated to end up on that album. It was therapy, and I needed it. While he was inside, we'd write—always letters, cards with shit like 'I love ya man,' and 'Can't wait to see you man,' and 'Stay strong, we gonna keep this going.' And that connection ended up, at least musically, keeping his spirit alive from what he told me later. It kept him going, because he got letters from tons of people, but I know it touched him that he got regular letters from me because of our musical connection. Then as soon as he was out of jail, it was like a day later, I didn't even know he was out, but Suge bailed him out, and I think his plane had landed and he'd just gotten settled into his Suite or wherever Suge had him put up at first. So two days fresh out of jail, I get a call from Big Syke, saying 'Someone wants to talk to you.' And I was—all nonchalantly like, 'Who is it? What's the fucking joke?' Then here comes this voice, 'I need you in the studio man, I'm out of jail. Meet me at the studio, I'm on Death Row.' And I couldn't believe it, I'm like 'Who the fuck is this?' And he's like 'Its Tupac motherfucker, get to the studio!' And we just got right back to work, banging them songs out."

Tupac's work ethic was legendary within his inner circle at Death Row, and would begin to become publicly recognized when the rapper emerged with hip hop's first double-album only a few months after his incarceration had ended. Prior thereto, Johnny J and Tupac were busy testing just how refined Death Row's well-oiled money machine would was, turning its massive wheels, burning the mid-night candle, and literally churning out song after song at a pace that the industry had never before witnessed. It was a true renaissance, equal only to Tupac's stature as hip hop's first renaissance rapper. As for all the hype that spewed out of the rap gossip-mill regarding the constant drama at Death Row rumored to go on in and out of the studio indiscriminately, be it rappers being pistol-whipped for using a studio phone or an engineer getting beat down for rewinding a tape to far, Johnny J for his part, recalled an artistically serene atmosphere that suggested just the opposite. Perhaps this was only because Tupac— irrefutably rap's biggest star at the time of his signing with Death Row—commanded such a working environment in order to accomplish the massive work schedule he had set for himself. In any event, as Johnny J recalled it, the bar that Shakur set at Death Row Records with his work ethic was one that the label respected at any cost, such that "once Pac was out, I can say this as a definite compliment to Suge, he definitely gave me and Tupac our space. Never interrupted, never tried to put his opinion in. I love the respect level of the way Suge approached things, even coming into the studio and vibing with me as I'm laying the track. Always loved the way I would track, and always loved the vibes and direction I was going into. The man had so much respect for the music I created that he even wanted me to start producing Danny Boy, Jewell, Snoop, you name it, the whole line-up. Suge looked at me and would say 'Man, you're like our Mexican Dr. Dre.' And I give him that much respect because he stayed on his side of the fence, and I stayed on my side of the fence doing my music. Another thing I know Suge loved was my and Pac's work ethic, because it matched his. He would always say, 'Man, your work ethics are unbelievable. You remind me of myself when I was in school.' One thing I'll say for Suge and Pac and I, with *All Eyez on Me*, we were dumping out so many songs at a rapid pace that it ended up becoming a double-CD by default almost. I remember Suge coming into the control room one night, and me and Pac were in there having a good time and next thing I know, he just made this announcement that it was going to be a Double CD, and became the first Double Album in rap history. He just said it right there on the spot."

While history may have been in the making with 'All Eyez on Me', there were certain stationary elements to Tupac and Johnny's collaboration that allowed them to work at the rapid pace they did, most of them among Tupac's vocal recording technique. While the signature method Shakur employed in recording his vocals was in and of itself unique to any other rapper in the game, the multi-tracking vocal style that Tupac practiced forced Johnny to stay constantly on his creative toes. As the producer explained the process for tracking a typical Tupac vocal session, "I had to know how to criticize myself at times and say 'I overproduced the record, I got a little too much going on, let me eliminate some shit, mute some things out, and open it up for Pac, so he could do what he needs to do.' Because he would lay a good 5, 6 vocal tracks, sometimes more than six. He really invented that style too, and it was a method of recording where he was thickening up the vocal quality, and also do subliminal stuff he could lay in the back of the song. Pac was known to do a main vocal, a double, then a triple that we'd call 'accenting' of certain things, where he would accent certain words. Then the fourth track we'd call the 'lollygaggin' vocal track, the 'fuck-around' track, things he wanted to say in the back, to talk a little shit while his vocal tracks were going. So I called the 4th track the 'talkin' shit' track, and when you hit that track, that was him laughing, giggling, responding to what he was saying. So that was pretty much our chemistry, and if you notice in the majority of every record I've done with him, the chemistry was always pretty much the same—vocally it was always structured pretty much the same: different topics, different melodies and formats, but structured out pretty much the same. Pac's thing when he was recording was always 'Give me a little reverb.' All he needed was a little reverb, always at all times. Didn't need delays, 'I need a gated reverb, I need this weird effect.'"

Still, for as stationary as Tupac's vocal recording style seemed, according to Johnny J, that very routine naturally allowed for experimentation to be built into any song as Shakur added layers, such that, when he was experimenting, "he loved the harmonizing effect, loved to go through a harmonizer, that was his favorite thing when I first met him. Cause then he would turn into the Freddie Krugar twins, he loved the Freddy Krugar voice. It was like a toy for him, the funnest thing to him. He was like a big kid with that. He was like a robot, that was when we first started off. Then there were times later on when it would turn into the high-pitched kiddy/woman voice, where he would do the woman parts in some songs, where he would actually speak out what the girl was going to say. He'd say 'All you need to do is high-pitch my voice J, make it sound real high, I'm gonna sound like a girl.' Cause at times when we were in the studio, there were no girls around, so we had no choice. And we wouldn't bring girls in to talk over the track, because it brought a comedic vibe to it, brought some real cool energy to it where it could make you laugh, even if he was talking on a real sensitive subject of what a female may be going through. But you could kind of giggle at what he was saying, and realize 'Oh my God, that is Tupac playing a female', because if you listened close enough you could tell it was his voice going through an effect to make his voice sound like a female voice. I loved that shit about him, he wasn't afraid to touch or try anything, and to take it to levels like that. He was creatively fearless. And I was too, so on all our collaborative levels, you could just hear that the chemistry was a locked-in deal, it was a marriage man, it was something that no one could break. Pac also raised my bar as a producer 10-fold, because when I'm producing, I always try to put myself in different shoes, and become the listener, and then the consumer, I think of myself as the regular, simple, typical street kid on a skate board or in my low rider, and just put myself in that position. And really think of myself on that level, of how these songs really put in effect on me. What vibe do they give me, what do they make me feel, what are they gonna make me do? What motivational aspect of things are…Where are they gonna take me to, these songs? Because I knew Pac's shit affected people like that. So it was a responsibility of mine. So I would put myself in those shoes. So I knew when he got out of jail, with the intensity and pace we were working at, we had alot of hungry motherfuckers listening for that next Tupac classic, so we just went in the studio and started banging them out."

Snapshots of Tupac

Chapter 7
The Recording of 'All Eyez on Me'

The recording sessions for 'All Eyez on Me', while they centered very much around Tupac and Johnny J's marathon recording sessions, also inspired the rest of the Death Row artist and production camp to jump on board for rap's most wildly creative roller coaster ride and rise to date at that time. There were no valleys as Tupac was very much at his creative peak with every song he laid down, with an indomitable spirit that informed the general mood of the sessions such that everyone attempted to push themselves to artistic parallel. Among the first producers to work with Tupac upon his release from prison, other than Johnny J, was another in-house Death Row producer and artist, Dat Nigga Daz, who produced 'Ambitionz as a Ridah', 'Skandalouz', 'Got My Mind Made Up', '2 Of Amerikaz Most Wanted', and 'I Aint Mad At Cha' with Pac for the album. Recalling for his part that "I was the (in-house Death Row) producer, I was dealing with him, Snoop Dogg, whoever the fuck you know what I mean? That's all I do, that's my job…I was (a) producer and he come to me every morning to get tracks you know? We Gemini's —we just keep it crackin like that and the same thing with the Outlawz…I'm (one of) the first (people) he hit when he went to Death Row we did six songs, all them songs went straight on his album at 11:30 at night and I started that. He got to Death Row and I was the first one to get in the studio with him." Recalling the specifics of one of the tracks he recorded with Tupac, Daz described the recording of 'Got My Mind Made Up'—a star-studded track that featured Inspectah

61

Deck, Method Man, Redman, and the Dogg Pound—as a laid-back affair that unfolded "at my house. Kurupt had brought Method Man and Redman over to my house. And Inspectah Deck was on the song too. He was at the end —'I.N.S., the rebel...' Just his voice. They had taken his voice. They had taken his verse out and kept the background 'cause it sounded good....(Tupac was) flossing like, 'I got a beat with Method man, Redman.'"

Another guest on the song, Death Row artist Kurupt recalled that the beat was so hot, initially everyone was after it, such that "the original record was me, Rage, Redman, Method Man and Daz. I told Daz, 'Man, this is the one, we need to drop this, we need to put this on Dogg Food.' 'Cause we did it when we was making Dogg Food. When 'Pac came home, we put it up for 'Pac, like 'You want this record?' Pac was like 'Hell, yeah, I want that record!' And he dropped his verse where Rage's was, 'cause Rage said she'd put her verse on something else, and that's how that record made it on 'Pac's album. Me, Method Man and Redman and Daz and Rage —that was the original record, and Inspectah Deck was on it at the end. That's him you hear at the end: 'Wish...this...bliss...' That's inspectah Deck. I went and picked up Red and Meth and Deck personally and took them to Daz's house. We knocked the record off in about three, four hours. It was a done deal, and then we...we didn't use it, 'cause Daz wasn't feeling like mixing it and doing all that. We end up taking it to 'Pac when 'Pac came 'cause Suge was like, 'When it's time to work on a project, everybody needs to give everything to whoever's project it is.'" Yet another Daz-produced track, 'Two of Amerikaz Most Wanted', which also featured Snoop Dogg, popped off in the same impromptu manner as all of the non-Johnny J produced tracks seemed to transpire, wherein the talent potency among the Death Row artist pool was the only thing that kept the sessions from seeming rushed or disorderly. The method to Tupac's madness, as engineer Rick Clifford captured it during the recording of the aforementioned track, was one in which "Pac was very adamant that the album was spontaneous. Everything that you hear, everybody got one take. They couldn't go back and fix anything. Pac said that number one, hip-hop is different from R&B. If a guy can't get out and spit eight to 16 bars, he's not ready yet. Then he said he loves the first take because there's a certain feel to it. He said if people go back and try and fix it, they would start thinking about it, they would lose the feel, they would mess it up. So the only one who refused to get out there like that was Snoop. Snoop said he'd come back tomorrow and do it. I think Snoop went home and wrote his stuff, learned his stuff, came in and knocked it off, first take. All Snoop said was, 'Wait a minute. You ain't going to put me out on one take. I'll come back and do it tomorrow.'"

Tupac's close friend and member of his Outlawz clique Big Syke recalls Tupac's attitude toward life upon his exit from prison and entry into the recording atmosphere surrounding 'All Eyez on Me' as one in which "when he came out of jail, all bullshit aside, it was all the same, he always had that drive in the studio. But see, when he got on Death Row, he had obligations to fulfill. He had shit that he had to do, to get the shit up and running, and so when he went to the studio, he was just taking care of business, and did all them songs. One thing though, when you go to the Penitentiary, you gonna grow up real quick. He didn't have no choice but to grow up, so he was more hard, but yet and still, he was still a kid at heart. We all kids at heart, wanna be young. As a rapper, Pac was Pac—he was always the hardest rapper. He always had them flows, I would hear his flows and go 'Oh shit.' But what it did with time was, he was able to see more, so he was able to speak on more. So through experience only do I think he grew as a rapper. He was the best before he went in, and still the best when he came out. Plus, I mean, if you at the studio all day, and you got all kinda cats there—from Nate Dogg, Daz, Kurupt, all those cats coming through, plus Johnny J—it just gonna keep you working. He always had it, but when he got at Death Row, he also had full access to the studio. 24-hour, round the clock access, to where he didn't have to have somebody book no studio time, or none of that. There was always a studio for you when you're ready, no matter what time you wanna go. Anybody was welcome to the studio, as long as you wasn't no fake motherfucker. If you knew somebody that he didn't know who was in the studio, he would never be like 'What he doin' in here?' I never heard him say some shit like that. Anybody he said that shit to was already gettin' they ass whooped. So it wasn't ever no problem. This was every day when he got out of jail: we would get up in the morning, because I lived with him at this suite at the Peninsula in Beverly Hills, for like 3 or 4 months straight. And we would get up every day, and by 12 noon we would be at the studio. We would usually leave the studio at around 10 o'clock at night and go to the club, every day."

"During those Death Row days, I stayed with his ass in a hotel for 4 months, and I had beach front property. I had a spot on the beach to go to, so I was there because he was my nigga. He wanted me there, so I'm gonna be witcha. He spent most of the time with his folks, and then late night, get with a woman. That was how his life went mostly. Day time: he's handling business with his niggaz. Night time: 'Okay, come on ladies.' Anybody who know him know he wasn't spending no day time with chicks, he was with his niggaz 90% of the time. Then if was wasn't going to the studio, or he wasn't on a movie set or whatever, we was out shooting paintballs, all kind of shit, having fun, enjoying life. So in the studio, there was always something to do. He might do two songs, then start a third and let everybody else get on a song. He had one or two he that he's gonna knock out, that he planned for himself, then there's extra beats around, so now we can all get in on it. Long as we keep working, it's all great. He always kept working. It was like that during the Thug Life sessions, at all the sessions was like a party, but we working. We'd get loaded, we smoking, but we ain't about to stop working, at no time. That was his ethic. At all times. That's why, even when we got to Death Row, to me it wasn't nothing different. There wasn't nothing different going on because

Pac was doing the same damn thing—working. That's what I knew him for, I knew him to go to the studio to do what he gotta do to get up out of there."

Another producer who Pac called upon had midas lineage, descending from one of America's Jazz greats, was QDIII (a.k.a. Quincy Jones III), who recalled that Tupac's work pace and implied talent therein took him by storm, such that "before I met (Tupac) I didn't really think too much of him because he was always running his mouth and acting out of control. But when I heard 'Dear Mama' I realized that he was one of the first rappers that did a song that had real emotion that really moved me. At that point I started diggin' his music and after he got out of jail I contacted him and asked him if the album was done and he said yes but let me hear what you got. I gave him a beat tape with "Heaven Ain't Hard To Find" and he said that's just what I need right now and he ended up taking a song off of 'All Eyes..' and adding 'Heaven...' And he wrote it so quick and he was so cool and real that over night I under stood that he had a special gift that I had never witnessed anything like before in all my times as a rap producer." Offering further insight from a producer's insight into the method moving Tupac's creative brilliance in the booth, QDIII observed in the course of working with the rapper that "Pac was a first mind type of person, by that I mean he listened to what ever came to his mind first and went with it so just being around him and seeing him write so quick or make important decisions in a heartbeat was always impressive non stop...He was just trying to be as real with people as possible without bullshit and if they couldn't take it he didn't care, you gotta' respect that."

Also witness to the Tupac's wonder work ethic during the recording sessions for 'All Eyez on Me' was engineer Dave Aron, who worked the boards in support of a variety of producers for tracks. Recalling the atmosphere surrounding the recording of the album's debut track, 'Ambitionz As a Ridah' as a sign of what Tupac had in mind thematically for his tenure with Death Row,

Aron recalled that "that's the first song I ever did with Tupac. The day he got out of jail, he didn't go to the clubs. He didn't go try to meet women. He went straight to the studio like he was on a mission, and he recorded 'Ambitionz Az A Ridah.'…Tupac came in, and he was fresh out of jail. I seen them give him his Death Row medallion that same night. And then he came right in. He was ready to go. He was very hyped, very focused, a lot of energy —mad energy. And you could tell he was really one a mission. He really had a real vision of what was going on, and he wanted to get a lot done in that short amount of time." Dat Nigga Daz, who produced the song, remembered that the musical soundscape was inspired by "me sampling Pee Wee Herman. So if you listen to Pee Wee Herman (the Champs' 'Tequila'), I just put the gangsta twist on it. I gave it to 'Pac. Came back to the studio, and it was done." Kurupt, for his part, echoed the broad sentiment that Tupac raised everyone's ambitions as players on Death Row's team of artists, such that "(the) first day he came home…Suge brought him in. The word went through the office that 'Pac was home. Everybody (who was) at the studio at that time were up there. I came a little bit later, and when I came, Daz already had the beat (for 'Ambitionz as a Ridah') started. Pac wasn't in the studio for any more than 45 minutes before he had his first verse done and laid. That fast. He didn't even wanna chill; all he wanted to do was get on the mic. Whatever day he landed in Los Angeles, two hours after he landed, he had his first verse laid."

Other producers who Tupac called upon to contribute one-off tracks to the All Eyez on Me sessions included Rick Rock, who produced 'Tradin' War Stories' alongside partner Mike Mosley. Rock recalled that his collaboration with Tupac was very much in the moment, so much so that "I don't know where the fuck I got the sample from. Dionne Warwick or something. When I ended up doing it with 'Pac, I told him it was 'It's A Man's World.' And it got cleared under that, but I don't know who it was. I know I didn't get it from James Brown. I got it from somewhere else, but it sounds like, 'A Man's World.' I couldn't remember, 'cause I used to do beats and I didn't keep my samples. I just had all my shit on a disk. And when I came to California from Alabama, I used to carry a bag full of disks." Shakur also enlisted Jodeci mastermind Devante Swing to produce 'No More Pain', a session which engineer Dave Aron recalls as one in which "I was at the studio at 8 late—10, 11 p.m. At 3 a.m. DeVante showed up by himself. He wanted to lay a few more parts before they mixed it. It was a very sparse track. But the keyboard parts he put in were very eerie and weird sounding. He was very quiet that night. Very focused. It was interesting to watch him work. He finished about five or six in the morning and said, 'I want to mix this now.' We mixed it that same night. It was a long night."

Another classic from the album, 'Only God Can Judge Me', was produced by Doug Rasheed alongside Harold Scrap Freddie, and again engineered by Dave Aron. The engineer recalled this track as being among Tupac's most personal, such that "I thought that was pretty introspective. Pretty straightforward. (Doug Rasheed's) beats weren't that complex. They usually were comprised of a few loops and some percussion and a good solid drumbeat." Another track that came out of these one-off sessions was 'When We Ride', produced by DJ Pooh, which formally introduced the world to Tupac's crew, the Outlaw Immortalz. The producer recalled that the session for this track unfolded spontaneously, such that "we were over at Can-Am Studios working on a bunch of material. It was me, Soopafly, Daz, all the producers—we're just sitting there working out tracks. Tupac, Dre and Snoop Dogg—all the artists were going through the studio checking out tracks and recording songs. It was like a work machine. It was one of the best scenarios any record company would want to see. All these powerful people in the studio working together. And Tupac also brought along his crew. Guys always want to open the door for cats that's coming behind them. He was opening up the door for the Thug Life cats then. I had a track that 'Pac came in and was like, 'Whoa, what the fuck is this?' I was just twisting it together. He was like, 'This is us!

We doing it! We're going in the other room. When we finish up over there, we'll be over here tonight.' I said, 'Okay.' Later on, I guess early in the morning, three or four in the morning, he stepped into the studio and said, 'Put that track back up!' I put the track back up, and he instantly was like, 'This is the one that we doing with the group—we gonna ride on this one and ride the track.' 'When We Ride.' He came up with the hook right there and just laid the hook down. He had all the guys come in one by one and just kick it off. It was incredible, man. The song was done in a couple hours. In one night everybody felt like they just wanted to take a crack at it —just jump on it, go spit. So many different flavors and styles —it was an incredible opportunity."

West Coast local rap legend DJ Quik was also a favorite of Tupac's, and as part of the family, was brought in by the rapper to contribute the track 'Heartz of Men' to the double-album epic the rapper had undertaken. Quik recalled that his professional name-sake spoke aptly for the momentum surrounding all manner of goings-on at camp Death Row in those days, such that, as a producer, "a lot of the credits got fucked up back then. It was real bad businesses going on up there sometimes, and if you didn't go into the office with Roy Tesfay (Suge Knight's assistant) and them and you do your credits, you got screwed. I got fucked. I did a lot of remixing on that record, and overdubbing and mixing (that I wasn't credited for). I made a lot of those records sound a lot better than they did when they came into the studio, and it a real small amount of time. In two days, I remixed like 12 songs…(So) the credit system in the Death Row days was like if you weren't strong about getting your credits somebody would take your credits from you. If I didn't go to the meeting or the office and put my name down on the album, I couldn't expect somebody to do it for me. Somebody would lie and say they did the work because they know it might make them look good to Suge or they might get some work off of it and that's what happened to me…I helped with the 2Pac "All Eyez On Me" a whole lot…(But) somebody took one of my credits and claimed he mixed the song that I produced for 2pac. Nobody mixes songs that I produce except me or an engineer that I deem worthy of mixing it."

With respect to the one song DJ Quik was credited with producing on 'All Eyez on Me', albeit under his birth name David Blake rather than his professional moniker, Quik recalled that the interworkings of their collaborative process as "Tupac…venting. He was vexed about something he wanted to speak about and my job as the producer is to lay down the musical bed so he can be most comfortable getting that shit out of his system. And I think that's what we accomplished. A driving, angry beat to match his driving, angry delivery…We'd get into it every now and then. He'd be like, 'Fuck Quik, why you gotta be so hard on me with the backgrounds?' I'm like. 'If you make them perfect, they'll always be perfect. But if you just slouch, they're gonna suck forever.'" While DJ Quik felt he had to hold Tupac to his own bar in being fearless as a producer in spite of Tupac's celebrity—speaking up when he felt the rapper needed to correct something—the producer explained that he did so for the sake of the legacy he felt morphing in both their presence, such that "Pac was a consummate artist. Pac would really think first before he wrote. He would become a part of the song. Almost as if he knew the shit would last forever. He was that meticulous about the way he wrote to certain tracks. My thing with that record was that, as tight as Tupac was —he's legendary —I still had to be the producer and check what I didn't like and how we could make that record near perfect, if we couldn't make it perfect. I had to be stern with him one some things, but for the most part, it was like he was a ghost. It was like, 'You're not supposed to be here.' He was there in the flesh."

Quik also felt Tupac took his creative direction where it was offered well, namely because, as the producer saw it, "I know that he respected me because I was older and then after we worked together I think he respected me because of me, David Blake. I showed him a couple of things that he probably didn't know, but that I made apparent to him." Still, the producer is, well, *quick* to acknowledge that the tutelage was mutual, such that "he accepted what I had to show him and I accepted what he had to show me. What he showed me was a tenacity that I could probably never have as a rapper when it comes to microphones and getting off your chest what's on it. The muthafuckin' boy could write probably 5 songs a day and I'm not exaggerating. This muthafucker was incredibly crazy when it came to raw literature…I learned from Tupac that if you totally just open up, the light will shine right thru you. You'll be illuminated because ya let the bullshit roll off your back and if you have to beef, ya know everything he did, he did like a thousand percent. I mean he was like a motorcycle fully wide open; but he was also bright. Ya know what I mean; he was like illuminated. Uninhibited and that is what I learned from him to be uninhibited." The latter was perhaps among the best single ways to describe the atmosphere surrounding the recording sessions for 'All Eyez on Me', completely uninhibited and free of pressure other than that which Tupac applied as his own standard, and that by which anyone and everyone else around him, either deliberately or by default, was made to follow. Because of Death Row's ocean-deep pockets, there were no suits watching the clock, although from the sounds of it, Tupac ran a tighter ship than any coach ever could have for his team of players on the project. Excellence was the foundation of the level Tupac operated at, and he expected nothing less of himself and all around him who he involved in his creative process. While many producers worked with Tupac during this period, most collaborated with Shakur in a one-off capacity, or over the course of a session or two wherein 5 or 6 songs were produced, which was Tupac's M.O. for any given day in the lab. There was only one producer who Tupac seemed to trust implicitly, and that was Johnny J. If confirmed by no other fact than the sheer amount of material the two recorded together over the last year of Tupac's life. Beginning with 'All Eyez on Me' and beyond, when Shakur got home from jail, between the two of them, it was on.

Chapter 8
Tupac and Johnny J Take Over...

There have been many in the course of the historical analysis of Tupac's legacy, specific to his image and its metamorphosis over the course of his rise to hip hop's pinnacle between 1991 and 1995 when he joined Death Row and went completely gangsta. As Johnny J saw it, knowing Tupac both before and after his stint in Clinton Correctional, nothing changed about the fabric of Tupac personally other than those ways in which the experiences he had gone through in real time with his career had matured him—both as an artist and a man. That coupled with the fact that, upon his release on bail, the East Coast-West Coast beef was fully on, Tupac felt an obligation to rep for the West Coast on a level and in a position that no other emcee at the time had enough individual juice to command. Therein, the burden was Tupac's, and as Johnny J remembered, in spite of this new responsibility professionally, nothing changed between their personal dynamic creatively. If anything, as the producer recalled, it involved because they both were charged with the responsibility of raising the West Coast collectively to a superior level on Tupac's shoulders, such that "on 'All Eyez on Me', Pac—even before he was around Suge and Death Row, he was a mouth piece for hard core shit. He loved to bounce around on different vibes, but he had to speak up, because he was a spokesperson for street thugs. For the pimps, the players, however you want to call it. So when he got to Death Row, he had to bring that aggressive approach because it was Death Row Records, but I love Pac for the fact that he did keep the sensitive side of things on the record too. And that got respect from the label too, without a doubt. That's another thing I loved about me and Tupac once he was on the Row, because we weren't afraid to keep the chemistry we had before he got to Death Row, we kept it the same even at Death Row."

The latter is extremely important to understanding Tupac's broader appeal beyond the rough necks because he spoke equally for their ladies. Tupac's voice was the scripture written from a million cries of struggle, perhaps metaphorically captured in his multi-tracking vocal recording style—but for as often as he brought the harder tone to his songs for the street soldiers, he also held the hopes and dreams of a generation of women who needed equally as passionate an advocate to speak on their behalf. In that respect, Tupac was really the first male rapper to speak up for women on a commercial level, through pre-Death Row hits like 'Brenda's Got a Baby', 'Keep Ya Head Up', and 'Dear Mama', and in a revelation that may surprise some of Shakur's fans, as Johnny J told it, "if you want to know the truth, the emotional, sad songs were his personal favorites. There was just this emotional state or reminiscent vibe he would get about what little mama was going through, whoever. So the man would get quiet for a minute, and start biting on his lip, and thinking about the struggle Afeni had been through, or all black women universally—having a baby at young age, going through the struggles—and that's how he had come out with 'Keep Your Head Up' and 'Dear Mama' before we got together, and afterward, songs like 'Mama's Just A Little Girl', or 'Wonder Why They Call You Bitch.' And it would always start with me, it would start with the instrumental, it was like a punch to the face, and Pac would be like 'Aw man, as soon as Johnny played that, I knew where I wanted to go.' In the vibe of any of his spiritual records or sad songs, he never cried in front of me, but you could see a change in his attitude and body language, to where you could see something was emotionally touching him. So you could see the pain through the body language, the whole vibe of it, where he would kind of mellow out, and you'd see him stuck in thought. And we would all get in that mode. There were times when we would hit those records, where we would hit home so much or touch down on a serious subject like 'Life Goes On' or 'Better Days' where it would literally make guys walk out of the studio watered up and crying. We actually made hard core guys, from the street, walk out of the studio in tears. Suge loved them, I didn't see him cry, but I could see that he definitely loved emotional records. I do recall that 'Life Goes On' was definitely one of his favorites…We had people in (that session that you'd call) street guys or hardcore, they were deep into their thing and they broke down in tears. I can't believe I saw that. (That record) just had so many people emotional." Another studio regular who contributed back-up vocals to several songs on 'All Eyez on Me', Dru Down, was present for the writing and recording of 'Life Goes On', and recalled that "(that tune) was more on the serious tip. When (Pac and Johnny J) got serious about something, there wasn't too many people up in the studio. When a nigga wanna really be serious, 'Pac just dumped out all the weed on the mixing board —about four ounces of smoke —and was writing. And niggas had to be quiet. It was on the real low, quiet tip. That was a serious time."

In exploring the specifics of the chemistry between Tupac as a recording artist and Johnny J as a producer, Johnny's production style must be examined musically to understand the foundation it laid for Tupac lyrically. In that context, Johnny explains that his process for building any instrumental begins with an innate sense on his part of what people will do while they're listening to his tracks, such that "when I'm at a nightclub, at a restaurant, or out wherever, I'll look at people's reactions when a song is playing, I can look at the vibes and trip off what people react to, and I'm just like this: I'll hear people humming melodies and singing different things, and on the radio, just to see where their heads are at, and it really gives you an idea, as a producer, of where you need to be in music, where it needs to be. You can tell what's catchy. So I'll just think to myself 'Look at how people can just hum shit or sing shit in the grocery store,' and I can be right there grabbing the milk and eggs with the wife, and hear people singing these songs, and it just goes to show you how shit can grow on people. I'm just observant like that. That's the vibe I like to go after on my records."

Delving into some of the technical aspects of his process for constructing a musical soundscape, Johnny explains that "when I'm building a track, from the time I first started producing to this day, the SB1200 is always going to be a part of my musical chemistry, until the day I leave this earth, because if it ain't broke, don't fix it. Every drum track known to man on every song I've done since the day I started producing records has always been that drum machine. I'm a drummer, I was originally on the drums, and can play the hell out of the drums. Keyboards, you name it, I can play it all, have dealt with it all, I was a serious rhythm guy, serious percussionist, very into the marching band thing during junior high and high school. I've always had to do my thing on the rhythms, couldn't stop beating on the desk in elementary school, I used to get in trouble. The teacher was always like 'Thank you for the entertainment, you can go to the corner now.' Little Ricky Ricardo was in the making, I am the original Ricky Ricardo. The reincarnation of Ricky, and my wife is Lucy. So whenever I was doing my marching in high school, even before I'd ever seen the inside of a recording studio, I was always curious about how records were created, how does this stuff go on the vinyl. How does this process start? So while I was in high school, I started asking alot of questions, and that's when the relationship started with the Candyman record 'Knockin' Boots', where we entered the recording studio due to the fact that someone wanted to invest in a record label, and I got introduced to a home studio. Some simple equipment—some drum machines, at the time there was the Roland 808, the TR808, which was my favorite drum machine until the SB12 came out, which you had to hook a separate disc drive to, which was like a dinosaur to me. But I got through it, and then when the SB1200 entered the game around 1990, I knew that was my calling. That was all she wrote, and 'Knockin' Boots' came out of that drum machine."

Elaborating, Johnny explains that "my process for building a track was always this: my chemistry always began with sitting there and figuring out how the drums should go. I would always start with the drum track, I never sang a melody to myself yet, never thought about where I wanted to take a bass line, or any chords, nothing like that. I had to make sure that the foundation started with the drum track. Mandatory for me, to make sure the kick, the snare, the high hat was on point, the actual pattern, where every simple element was going to go, then I'd just layer it up. Go into the bassline mode, go into the chords, which I would always foundation off the Fender Rhodes, and just do my thing. Just build and build till I couldn't build anymore. I love the Fender, I'm a (mini-mood guy), I love the mini-moods, I love the old school instruments. For bass, I was always using the (Kirkswell), (Kirkswell) is still a part of my musical chemistry to this day, don't ever plan to change that. Everybody's always...as soon as one keyboard's been popular, its like 'Okay, that's a wrap for that one, there's a new introduction, another one out.' I never liked to jump on the bandwagon, and follow the trend of what everybody does. Its like jumping onto a new pair of shoes, sometimes you need to know how to keep the same shit on, just keep it clean, and know what you're doing. Some people think 'Yo, if I buy this new keyboard, it's going to make a hit record.' No, its called 'Motherfucker, if you know you have a musical ability, and how to create melody and concepts that are going to ring in people's ears, that's where it starts my friend.' It doesn't come out of some new keyboard you bought, it comes out of your heart, and your musical background. And my musical background includes every soul record you could possibly think of, even Mariachi music, Latin music—you name it—it was in my upbringing. You hear Jazz in my background. In some situations, I'll use sampling. A good example would be a song called 'Ballad of a Dead Soldier.' That was one I did based off of a Curtis Mayfield sample. So I would vibe off the way it was structured, and most of us at the time who would sample would listen to an 8-bar intro of an old record, or an old classic 70s song. And that song by Curtis Mayfield actually was from the beginning of the record, but what I would usually do that set me apart is: I would take the middle of the song, or wherever, and dissect it just out of some weird place. But once I take a sample, whether it be from the beginning, middle or end of a song, I would structure it out, dump it into my sampler, and loop it for a good 4-8 bars. I was always good at sampling 4-8 bars, some producers would do a 2-bar loop. It was rare that I would do a 2-bar loop, but I was good at looping a 4-8 bar sample. So once I had sampled, I'd start knocking drums out right away. I'd go right into my kick, my kick drum would go right into it immediately. And I was always known to keep an 808 Kick Drum in all my records, and I don't know if you know this, but all of the records I produce consist of an 808 kick drum blended into the mix. That's mine as a trade-mark, you always put your little boom on, and mine was the 808. It just always kept a good frequency, a good theme in all the records I've produced. And I don't know what it is about me, but I just have to have that in all my songs. Every record, every single song. I'm good at blending it, because you might not always hear it as loud as in other cuts, but it would always put a nice tone, a nice texture to the majority of my tracks."

Continuing, Johnny explains that "I would start building off the samples, and then just layer it and layer it and layer it. We kept the musical elements in the studio at all times—such as the guitar player, and the keyboardist—I don't care if we had to have horns in there, or a violinist or string section. Whatever it took, we always had the musicians in the studio with us at the time we were recording. I would have to guide them through what I wanted them to play, because most of them are musicians, not producers—so they would follow my lead, and play whatever I told them to play. Or even Tupac, he might sing a little melody or two, or hum a few lines, and the guitar player would go off that, and take it into another fade. Then I might say 'Naw Pac, watch this—let me take it to another level.' Then I'd guide the guitar player to another fade, and that's another layer of the track that would go on top of the sample. Then I'd look at the keyboard player, like 'Now, this is what I want you to do on the chords. I want you to structure the chords this way. I want you to use these sounds for the chords…' Whether it be a Rhodes, or whether it be a straight sound, or some weird Clavonette type of sound. Then I'd go into the mini-mood, and I'd say 'Let me get this high-pitched UFO sound, and do something real weird with it.' It wouldn't always have to be Parliment Funkadelic style, I would just do something real spacy and shit, something psychedelic about it. I would just do shit like that, hit the weirdest note that would be in key on the mini-mood, and the shit just worked. And I'd keep it. And just build layer upon layer upon layer. So by the time we got to his vocals, we'd musically have staked up—from the kick to the snare to the high hat, all the percussion to the guitar, keyboards, bass, and what—and those were on separate tracks. I'd say there was a good 16 tracks, and we'd work on a 48 tracks, because we had two 2-inch machines linked together. This was before Pro-tools, so we were working on the dinosaur of the time, we were just dumping the shit on 48 tracks. So I'd say about a good 16 tracks before we got to vocals, but if I needed a 17th track or an 18th track, musically they were open for me to use."

"Because I wasn't the type of producer that—just because you got 48 tracks in front of you, it doesn't mean you have to fill every fucking track. You got to be a fucking idiot to produce records that way. Just know when to call it, by the 30th track or whatever, most times it's a done-deal, a wrap. My advice on that point is you gotta keep it simple, simplicity is the key. Everyone has said that expression I'm sure throughout the music industry, but truthfully it's always been the key for me. You have to know when not to overproduce records. You need to know when to say 'Let me lay out a basic structure of where I want to go with my music,' and get some vocals done, and let the vocalist get their thing done, whatever they feel they needed to get off their chest. Then get a working vocal mix and build around that, then you can make the musical concept happen even better. Say, for instance, I've laid the drum track, I laid the bass line, the chords are laid out, and maybe just a simple melody line. And alot of times, I wouldn't have a melody line yet at that point because my melody line might clash with what the artist is trying to write. They may sing something totally different that may go against what I'm trying to create for a melody, so I don't like to put melody lines on records too much till vocals are done. I'm good at knowing how to work around the vocals, you gotta know how to respect the vocalist too. You can't be like 'I'm the producer, I'm the music guy, so I have to shine.' You have to know how to say Fuck that, it has to be a 50/50 thing, right down the middle. Sometimes you gotta know when to back off—as a musician and as a producer—and say 'You know what, I kinda overproduced it, I put a little too much on it. I'm getting a little too musically keyboard happy on my fucking song.' And so I would take some of the excess elements off to show a little more respect for the vocals that were on the song, and make it sound a little more like a properly-arranged record. As a producer, another very important thing is to know how to arrange your elements. Know when to bring in your elements, know when to take them out. It's having a musical gift and a musical knowledge to know how to create original music also, because I don't sample anymore. You can be inspired by an old record, but still—as a new or established producer—think to yourself 'Let me originate something that's going to be classic, and a memory until the end of time.'"

Unique to many producers, Johnny had the ability to come into a given recording session with instrumentals already completed which in turn would inspire the lyrical direction in which Tupac took the song. Conversely, he could also build the track from the ground up in real time with a lyrical or melody idea that might have originated in Tupac's mind absent any suggestion or influence on Johnny's part. On this level, the creative interplay was superior to most standard methods for recording hip hop emcees, wherein the artist came in and wrote a rap to an already-completed instrumental, let alone for the rapper to play a role in steering the song's musical direction. As Johnny J recalled this element of Shakur's multi-faceted talent as a recording artist, "Pac, as a recording artist, I would definitely consider musical outside of rhyming. I loved the fact that I didn't have to sit there and get frustrated on the fact that he didn't know how to come into the song, or couldn't understand what 16 bars were. He knew all that, but I would still actually sit there and count as he would recite the vocals in the booth, to let him know that's 16 bars and that's enough. So he would look at me with my cues, and I'd count him down, 'That's 16, stop there, its time for hook.' There were times when Pac was so good, when his rhythm was so together, that it was an automatic program. The majority of his records were always 16 bar verses then hooks, and it just came together. And I loved it because he just knew how to form a different type of rhythm on top of my beat, that you wouldn't think would work, but it worked. It was like this off-beat style he would do in his doubles or triples in his vocals, and it would just come in out of nowhere, and you'd be like 'Wait a minute, what the fuck was that?' Then you'd listen back like 'Oh shit, it does work.'"

In this regard, the way in which Johnny and Tupac build their tracks remained naturally spontaneous in that, as the producer recalled it, "the way we usually worked was—if I had the track pre-produced at home, I would bring it in with me that day to the studio, pop it in, and he would write it right there on the spot. There was NEVER an occasion that I can remember, where he brought me lyrics, showed me lyrics, then I put a beat to it. Every song we recorded, from song number one to the last song we done, was always written on the spot. Never brought a piece of paper out of his back pocket, never pulled out nothing talking about 'I wrote this at home' or 'I wrote this at the hotel', he went off the experience he had the night before. Whatever he dealt with the day before or the night before, that was pretty much the experience he'd walk into the studio with. That's how we ended up doing 'Check Out Time', from a Las Vegas experience. Whatever he had dealt with, whatever was going down that day would pretty much become the subject for the songs we recorded that night. 'I went to Roscoe's, I did this, I ran into some females, I see the same ho everywhere I go.' That became 'All About You.' I think the corollary between how he rapped in the moment and lived his life in the moment was very naturally the way he preferred things. He didn't try to do it that way, planned—so it was always a natural vibe, of what you felt right there on the spot. I loved the way it all came out, and not everybody could come into the studio with a subject, and just write a whole song right there on the spot. Not everybody has that gift. And when I didn't bring something in from home already prepped, I would make up my beats right there on the spot with him, which was most of the time. We had it that naturally with each other, we were that in synch…That was one of the most hilarious records I've ever done with Tupac…I used Cameo's old school cut (1986 single, 'Candy'). Nate Dogg, Snoop, everybody sitting around on speakers, doing their thing."

"Next thing I know (Nate Dogg sings): 'Every other city we go. Every other video.' I'm like, 'Nate, I know you gotta be fucking playing.' They're like, 'Nah, man. We're dead serious. That's the hook—we're talking about video hoes.' Nate Dogg, for his part, recalled that "it was me, (Pac) and Snoop, and we were talking about all the girls that we had seen before. The whole thing came from a video shoot. We were at a video shoot, and it was so funny how, if it wasn't Snoop that knew the girl, Tupac knew her, or I knew her. It's like, 'Damn, everywhere we go, we see the same girls.' And that's how the song came about. It was the same as it always is: A little liquor, a little weed, we aiight. 'Pac was one-taking his verses. He did that a lot. We were having so much fun, the song just came out." Also present for the session in which 'All About You' was recorded, vocalist Dru Down remembered that "it was me, 'Pac, Syke, Rage and a couple of Outlawz in the studio. We always had bitches in the studio. The only thing crazy was, the Outlawz niggas—Fatal Hussein and Yafeu Fula—were gonna get on the track. It was like an interlude at the end. I did the beginning. They were gonna do something at the end. Then them muthafuckas did something where they fucked up. They couldn't get it right. They were too high and too drunk. They were messing up. They were in the microphone booth, and they were fucking up, and 'Pac said, 'Y'all gotta get the fuck up out of there. I don't know what the fuck y'all are doing.' They was just playing around. They were taking too long, wasting time. They laughed their ass up in there and all the way out."

While Tupac and Johnny J, because of the natural talent level they operated at, could afford to create in the moment without any real fixed rules other than pre-existing norms built into Tupac's recording process, with anyone else Shakur involved on his tracks, there were rules of conduct which the rapper insisted they adhere to strictly. Beginning with engineers, Johnny explained that "Pac's patience level was very short. If there was any little minor technical difficulty—say for instance the tape machine got stuck, or something went out on the board—he would get very highly frustrated. He never got frustrated at me, but he got very hot with the engineer. He would get very upset at the engineer. He had a high standard—if they didn't get shit done in due time, or if an engineer ever erased his vocal by accident, they were fired. When you deal with 2-inch analog, you can accidentally hit that record button and erase a vocal. And we encountered a couple of those moments. The story behind that shit is unbelievable—let's just say some engineers were replaced, because of stupid fucking shit like that. I didn't like that kind of sloppiness, if my kick was erased or his vocal was erased, aww man you stepped on some real fucked up ground right there. Where you had to seriously look at this asshole engineer and lay your damn kick drum again, or replace the 4-bars he just erased. I'm looking at him like 'I already laid the damn song. Now I have to redo this, redo that, cause you erased it.'"

"That shit pissed Tupac off, because it was Death Row—and there was a very high standard that was always maintained in the studio, even amid all the drama and controversy that happened outside the studio. In the booth, Pac was always the most disciplined, that's how he got so much done." The rapper was even more strict with rappers guesting on his tracks, which applied principally to his clique, 'The Outlawz', who were just trying out for the team, while Johnny and Tupac were already Letter-wearin' veterans. As Johnny J recalled the duo's approach to recording the Outlawz, "some of when Pac and I would have to coach the Outlawz was some of the most hilarious shit I'd ever seen, because these guys would go in and think they could lay the main vocal, lay the double, and knock it out as fast as Pac could. And there was no way in the world they could do it, it was impossible. It was the fun-niest shit when they'd try, and then I'd look at them like 'Look man, get your shit together dude. Make sure that when you're writing your verses, you know what the hell you're gonna say on your rhythms.' Because they would write so many words, and combine so many, and then try to rhyme them and fuck it up, that Pac would look at them in the booth and say 'Man, if you don't get your ass back out here and restructure that, you're off it.' Pac would edit them himself sometimes, and like end their verses for them. He would cut it off him damn self, like if they wrote too many bars, some of the dudes would write 24 bar verses, and it would be cut down to 8. Pac would look at me and go 'We know where that shit's going to end. Next rapper.' Because there were 10 or 12 people in that crew, it was a line-up, and he had to keep the organized."

"That was Pac being a giving person, he and I were both giving in a musical way. We were open to share our creativity with other rap artists, or vocalists, we'd open the doors. And there were definitely times when, with that whole street attitude coming into the studio, his crew didn't always take direction too well in the booth, which is a natural requirement of producing. So I'd have to turn to Pac, and say 'Man, it doesn't work too well, I don't like the way that sounds.' Pac as a co-producer, especially on any kind of vocal, we were the toughest vocal coaches you could ever imagine. Especially if he was working with the Outlawz, he was like 'If you don't hurry the fuck up, and get that verse out the way, your ass is not on the song.' So he would literally have to tell them, 'If you don't get your shit done within a 5 or 10 minute time frame, you can cancel your ass off the record. Your ass is not on it.' So that kept 'em on point, kept them on their feet. He was like that with everybody. Another thing I never had to do for Pac was set a click track, I just had to cue him in with a typical pattern of some high hats, and 'Here comes the song', and count him on in. Once you start him off, he's on his own, off and running. You never had to go 'Hey, you're drifting off, your rhythm's a little shaky, you're not on the right pattern.' Some people could get behind the beat, and not be on the track right in terms of following the actual structure of the music. That's where we had to guide some of the Outlawz, and kind of train them, and coach them on what to do. I never had to do that with Pac."

Tupac, in speaking to the Outlawz on the outset of the recording sessions for what later became 'Still I Rise', provided a fascinating insight into his own philosophy and method for recording in sum, explaining that "we only got two weeks to do this whole album. Completed, to mix it down and everything. We don't have time or the luxury to spend all this time doing one song. We don't have it. We have to somehow find a way to double-up on it. I did my whole album—I know it ain't all that—but I did my whole album, like 3 songs a day. Cause I was just laying it, rockin' it, then getting off. You cam mix it later, just have niggaz who love being in the studio all night...after the rappers leave n' shit...But for why we in here, we got 8 rappers and everyone drinking and smoking n' shit. Man, get that beat poppin', throw them niggaz on the track, catch everybody freestyling. Boom—the name of the song is whatever this nigga said his last word was. After we finish, we go in, everybody listen to it, be like 'This is the hook.' Go in there, lay the hook, if we don't like that hook, nigga lay another hook. Then come back out…that be the song."

In spite of the amount of coaching that Tupac and Johnny J had to do during the recording sessions that involved the Outlawz—given that most of the group's members were teenagers—it was easier to coach them because they were very much students who had no problem looking up to Tupac as a teacher. In this context, Johnny as a producer felt that Tupac's mentor relationship with the Outlawz made it much easier to get through the considerable amount of patience sometimes required to get the group's vocal tracks on tape. As Johnny qualifies the latter, he explains that "I would advise to all producers that you need to get to know the artist. Get to know where their heads are at, and guide them through the rhythm patterns, and teach them to learn to change rhythms. Stop doing everything on the same monkey-see-monkey-do kind of vibe. Take it somewhere different. And not every song, don't go too left field, but think of something that's a little different, unique that somebody could learn from. Where they might say 'Hey, that was a hell of a pattern that he vocally wrote for that song. You gotta give it up, the pattern of those vocals were structured out beautifully.'"

"So positive re-enforcement is always important too. That came into play heavily when Pac brought in the Outlawz to record, because they were all completely green to the studio. You definitely have to guide a person into the flow, and the direction they're gonna go on a song, because some people think they gotta growl and get fucking upset on every song, if its topically gangsta. That doesn't make any fucking sense, because then you get alot of artists out there who tend to sound the same fucking way on every record. It could be an abortion song, and the dude in the booth is fucking growling, like he's about to burn the house down. There is a humanity when you're recording with just-off-the-block rappers, where you have to pause the session, look at the person grunting behind that glass, and as a producer—structure out a tone, and whisper to them about which direction to take it into. Don't look at them and say 'You're kind of over the boundaries on that. You gotta soften it up a little bit on that one.' The relationship that Tupac had with the Outlawz personally allowed us to get all of that done alot more easily than we would have given the street attitude they all came in with, along with natural immaturity given their age, had they been any random artists off the block that we were trying to work with."

As much as Tupac expected the Outlawz to take direction from he and Johnny J, Shakur personally had a very short fuse for prolonged recording sessions, such that, as Johnny remembered, "honestly, I think I was the only producer he had where, I could tell him 'You need to do that vocal again, or redo that double,' without him saying 'Fuck you, get the fuck out of my studio.' Because he wouldn't allow no other producers to cut him off like that while he was flowing. That whole process of trust established itself pretty immediately too. I'mma be perfectly honest with you, the mothefucka was such a genius that it was very rare he'd even make a damn mistake. And his mistakes are on the records, but you can't ever tell because those mistakes honestly worked because they were naturally meant to be. So unless it was something really egregious, which with him it almost never was, I rarely had to ever say anything to him. It was just knowing that I could if I felt it was required. You hear some of the most glitchiest, funniest shit going on in a vocal track, and I would say 'Pac, I'm gonna keep it, I'm not gonna mute it, cause you're such a damn comedian.' So we'd just look at each other, and go 'Fuck it, let's keep it.'"

"When Pac was recording a song, he expected it to be definitely completed from a tracking aspect of things the same day—musically and vocally tracked and done. With Pac and I, the real secret to our chemistry was that I musically matched exactly with where he was coming from lyrically. We usually got it right the first time too, because it was very rare that Pac would have to do anything over. Pac was definitely not one for punching in, he did NOT like to punch into the middle of a song. He liked to do each vocal line in its own full take. And if he fucked something up, he had to start over, which he hated, so he rarely fucked something up. Because he did not like to punch in. Its not that he couldn't do it, he just thought it was a waste of studio time. It would have to be the most bubble-gum shit to punch in, because he was so straight from beginning to end that he didn't really ever have to punch in. The flow and dynamics of his vocals were so unique, it wouldn't have the same feel. And it was weird for him, it just didn't work. So he wasn't the one to start over, 'We gotta do it again, we gotta do this again.' And as a producer, I loved that about him, because it was very rare that we had to do it again. So as soon as the first track was laid, we'd be on the double immediately. Now there would be times too when he would lay the first two vocal tracks, then come back and listen to hear something in the first track he wanted to alter. He'd come around on the next pass in the second vocal track and fill in—say for instance when he laid his first vocal track that he do so much shit, let so much out, that he'd lose his breath and miss a couple words. You wouldn't catch the words, so rather than go back and punch-in to fill in some word he missed, he'd just leave those open spots for the double. And when he went to lay down his second vocal track, he'd do it in the double. And what he didn't get to fill in on his second vocal, he'd fill in the triple. So any missing word within the verse, he'd end up replacing on the double, triple, or fourth vocal, so he could care less about doing the main vocal over if he missed a word. That was the most unique thing about him, he just ended up filling the puzzle into each song his own way. It was just beautiful like that."

While Tupac expected an equally low tolerance for error out of Johnny J, where they gave perhaps a bit more leeway to the

Outlawz because the crew were so green, when it came to back-up singers, Tupac and Johnny as co-producers were MUCH less patient. Johnny explained the difference as one in which "when I'm tracking a vocal, specifically a backup vocal, I stay kind of firm on them, I don't get upset or frustrated or anything, but I stay a little aggressive, because I don't like to treat it real nice and sweet and cute. I don't care if you're the prettiest girl in the world with the most beautiful vocals, if you're not hitting the notes right and doing the shit the way its supposed to go, I'm gonna look at you like 'You got to go, the shit ain't gonna work.' I'm a stickler like that. Me and Tupac were known for that. Pac had no patience by the way, he loved singers—don't get me wrong—he loved to hear singers in the booth, doing what they supposed to be doing. But if they were time bandits, and taking forever to lay the simplest set of backgrounds, Pac and I had that look in each other's eye like 'We're about to tell her ass to come out the booth.'"

While Tupac felt there was no room for error in the vocal booth, he left plenty of space for spectators in the studio—so long as they were part of his inner-circle. Johnny J explained their presence as a creative stimuli of sorts for Tupac, such that "when we were recording, Pac loved the spectators. Honestly, it kept an energy in the room. But at the same time, we would block it out, any noise or any talking or any distraction was going on, he would block shit out so that you would look at him and think 'He's not paying any attention...' Even if there were so-called *groupies* around, you could tell his mindset was like 'I'm not even thinking about that right now, I'm focused on the shit I gotta do behind this microphone, because what I just wrote and created, I gotta make this happen.' And me musically, I was on the same page. And I'd say the majority of his and my sessions had a crowd in them. We had a few that were pretty much me, him and my wife, who is always with me, she's my ace, that's my right hand. So she was there always on a quiet vibe. I remember there was one time—it touched me man—that he waited on me, he didn't want to do any vocals or create any song until I got to the studio and laid a beat down, and I was running late due to some family shit. He really respected that. It really touched my heart, it gave me a thing where I felt like 'This man really cares, and cannot do anything till I get there.' He didn't want to do nothing till I touched down to lay the track. He wouldn't even say 'Let's pop up a drum track.' Because there was always equipment around, all my shit was right there. But he never knew how to work my shit, and didn't let anyone else try either. I remember one day he said 'Johnny, you know if I start fucking with your shit I'm gonna end up throwing it because I don't know how to work it.' We had all kind of inside jokes, but we always kept a crowd, it was our way of saying 'Shit, that's our audience dude.' We had some ground rules—I remember there were times where it would get a little too overcrowded with people who just wanted to come in there, hang out for no fucking reason. 'Oh, let's go in and drink up Tupac and Johnny's Hennessey, and leach on em, and keep pouring Crystal,' without ever having the decency to contribute to what we bought. And Pac and I noticed it together, because we were always the ones paying for the shit, and whenever we bought Champagne, we always paid for it together, and we noticed together we had people coming in the studio trying to take advantage, trying to get a free ride. And we didn't really appreciate it."

While Tupac and Johnny definitely kept a tightly-patrolled V.I.P. list enforced during their recording sessions, for those who were welcome, the party went-on non-stop, even amid Tupac's tireless recording sessions, further reinforcing the extremely heightened and enlightened level of talent he was operating at to be functional at all given the amount of substances he consumed at any given time. Echoing the latter, as Johnny recalled it, " Pac was sponsored by weed, and was sponsored by Hennessey too. Both of those things were mandatory at any given Tupac recording session—you had to have a cup of Hennessey and coke, and some Crystal mixed in at times. I didn't smoke blunts, it just wasn't me. That high wasn't a good high for me, the one time he finally convinced me to try it, I hit Pac's blunt, and my console—the SL9000, the board itself—that turned into the Star trek Enterprise. And I remember Pac saying 'Don't ever let Johnny smoke weed again!' I haven't touched it ever since that evening. As far as drinking, to be honest with you, we stayed tipsy through every record I recorded with him. We were under the influence, I'll put it that way to you. Pac, for his part, could do his thing—smoke whatever he wanted to smoke and drink whatever he wanted to drink—and still step into the booth and handle a song like he didn't have one drink at all. We knew on certain songs that he recorded when he'd had one drink too many, and I think the songs speak for themselves, such as 'Thug's Passion', we were all pretty drunk right there. It was just beautiful that I could lay my music without having to be drunk or whatever, lay it down on the 2-inch tape, and get tipsy afterward. I didn't need it for creative chemistry, like 'I need to have this cocktail or this drink to create this vibe.' I could tell you that me and Pac didn't need it, cause if we'd been in there completely sober—which at times we were—we'd still have created the most beautiful music ever. I looked at it as an atmosphere thing, enjoying the moment, getting the shit out naturally and letting it flow. And I loved it because our chemistry flowed naturally."

Chapter 9
How Do You Want It?—Tupac and Johnny J

As recording progressed on 'All Eyez on Me', Johnny knew something magic was in the works, such that "I really felt when the whole level of 'All Eyez on Me' was going, from song one to where we finished what we had to do, I knew history was in the making. I felt the energy because I felt like 'Oh, now here's my chance, here's my opportunity to let the world know musically who I am.' And now lyrically, Pac can let it be known where he's at, where his mind was at. And I loved that, and I did deeply feel that history was being made, I knew that it was going to be a huge album. I can really say that. I didn't have my doubts, I didn't look at it like it was going to be this typical, corny gangsta shit coming out of Death Row. Or the typical street record. I knew we had a winner because I knew every song we would touch on—even when we did 'Wonder Why They Call U Bitch' to 'Life Goes On,' just imagine how I felt musically with all those different styles we got to touch. I had 18 different songs on the album originally, but then we reduced it down to 11 out of the 27, because we ended up taking what was left over and assigning them to a future album, but it was Pac and my work that deemed that 'All Eyez on Me' would be a double album, and it was all meant to happen. It was all written, all written man and I mean that spiritually, on a real serious level."

Johnny and Tupac shared a mutual affinity for one track in particular off of those that ended up on 'All Eyez on Me'—'How Do You Want It'—that seemed to serve as a prophecy of sorts for the barnstorm of hits the duo would produce together during Tupac's time at Death Row. As Johnny recalled the process for recording the song that would become Tupac's biggest hit to date, the producer recalled that the secret to the song's success, in his mind, was its chorus, which was slow to come at first, such that "the original vocal hook was done differently before you heard it with KC and JoJo. The beat was done four years before it touched down and got to Pac. I went through a good 4 or 5 rappers with that track before I got to Tupac with it. And when I showed it to Tupac, and he goes 'Its gonna be called How Do You Want It.' So then next thing you know, he's writing the verses, and he comes up with this melody and these words, and starts singing 'How do you want it? How does it feel? Coming up as a nigga in the cash game, living in the fast lane.' So he goes in the booth and sings it himself, with no back-up singers there. This was before KC and JoJo were even thought about. And honestly, I liked it the way it was originally done with Tupac as the singer. He sang the hook, and the whole song lyrically and melody wise, was written by him. He probably couldn't sing the notes in key, but I knew exactly what notes he was trying to reach. He had it, he had that gift, where he knew the melody, where it needed to go. I tripped off that, he was more than just a rapper. So then we tried out some girls singing the background, which didn't work out too well because the key was totally off, the females didn't come to the level we needed it to be at. Pac and I even had a discussion, and were like 'Naw, that ain't gonna work, we don't like them, have to take the girls off.' Cause we tried another girl thing, with the same identical wording, same melodic pattern, everything you're hearing in the record was the same, it just didn't have the right feel with the females. So then Pac said 'Johnny, what do you think about Jodeci?' So I said 'Not a bad idea.' And at that time, everybody was around, it was a big family vibe at Death Row. And so when KC and JoJo showed up, we laid them down, and it was the last thing to go on the record, and was like icing on the cake. It made my day to the fullest." Elaborating on the recording of what would become Tupac's most massive hit to date, engineer Dave Aron recalled that "Danny Boy was originally on the hook. I already had it mixed. And at the last minute. 'Pac wanted to put K-Ci and JoJo on it."

Jodeci's K-Ci remembered that "one night we were sitting in the crib, and Suge Knight gave me a call, 'cause we real good friends with Death Row family and everything. They asked us would we like to do a song with 'Pac, and we were like, 'Hell yeah, why not?"' That's our boy. So we got in the studio that same night, actually, that we got the phone call. Man, we were just tripping in the studio, having fun. If y'all read between the lines, y'all know what we were doing up there. (We) had the girlies up in there, doing our thing. The song came out blazing. The funny part was at first, when 'Pac was trying to sing it, trying to teach us how it goes. I was like, 'I see where you're trying to go, 'Pac, but it's not sounding too good.' Anyway, then we heard him doing his rhyme, and we're like, 'Man, we got to rip this, because he came strong.'

While everyone involved with Tupac knew he would sell records based solely off the controversy that naturally and constantly surrounded him, his waters as a legitimate, singles-chart hitmaker were less tested, and he needed that jewel in his crown to truly take the throne as hip-hop's pinnacle emcee and icon. Moreover, everyone was gambling on the fact that Tupac could still deliver a hit, not knowing how his sexual assault conviction and prison term might have affected his audience. The stakes were high, and the success of 'How Do You Want It' would push Shakur over the top, allowing him the cross-over success required to truly rule both the pop and urban charts simultaneously. Death Row Records similarly needed that achievement in their own right to truly compete on a cross-over level with Bad Boy, and the success of the aforementioned single attained that status for Suge and Company. Johnny J, as a producer, was also launched into orbit with the success of the single, and as the producer recalled, "I truthfully did NOT know that was going to become the record it became, it was a 3 million selling single. A hell of a chart topper. Went number one on the charts. That was the most unbelievable feeling you will ever have as a producer. And with Pac, there were certain songs where, after we'd finished recording, he would call it and go 'This is it. This is going to be the one.' And with 'How Do You Want It', I didn't call it, and don't get me wrong, I didn't doubt the song, I knew it was a club banger, and an energetic record. But I remember my wife hearing it and going 'That's gonna be a hit.' And then look at it, # 1 on the Pop Charts. I remember that 'How Do You Want It' was definitely Suge's number one favorite on 'All Eyez on Me.' I remember as soon as 'All Eyez on Me' went number one, I got a call from Pac. He said 'Johnny, do you know we are number 1 baby?' To see your album at number one, it was a high, it was unbelievable. I remember when we had the release party for 'All Eyez on Me', we were all in Vegas at Club 662, and a DJ was instructed to put 'How Do You Want It' on, and Suge looked at him and said 'If you don't put it on, your ass is fired.' And it was unbelievable, when that song came on, it raised the fucking roof. When we finished that song, we would—a lot of times, and specifically on that song—give each other a hug, and be like 'Did we put it down or what? Did we bring that chemistry together or what?' We looked at each other like Batman and Robin, it was cool. You could just see his smirk, and whenever you could see that smile on Pac, you knew he was a happy man. We both just knew that it was a song that was meant to happen, and that it was gonna be a winner."

"It was funny too, because after 'How Do You Want It' went number one, I got what seemed to me like millions of calls on that, tons of them. I remember looking at some of the magazines, some of the ads, and my name was big as day, 'PRODUCED BY JOHNNY J.' Real nice and huge, and I knew that was Pac. It was funny too, because after the success of that single, I started getting calls from everybody in the business, which really just worked to reinforce how special what Pac and I had was, because I stayed even after that pretty exclusively working with him. Our collaboration was something I knew he didn't want to see broken up, even for a song. He was very protective about it, it was almost as though, he didn't mind me collaborating other rap artists, whether it was out of Death Row or whatever the case may be, but his thing was this: he felt as though I was *his* producer, and until he got to hear the tracks I created, he had to hear them first before they went to any other artist. And that was his and my agreement, and I respected that about him. I respected that about what he said, because he sat down with me and had a conversation, and said 'Your my producer, and I feel as though anything you create, I get first dibs at it.' And I said 'You know what man, you do. I'll give you that love.' And this was before he went to jail, and all during our relationship."

Reviews of 'All Eyez on Me' were a victory for Tupac following his year-long incarceration, as critics lapped endless praise on the first double-album in rap history, beginning with *Rolling Stone Magazine's* commentary that "2Pac shows more skill than most. He deserves to have all eyes—and ears—on him," while Rap Pages raved that "the lyrical Jesse James is back to expound on his lengthy dogmas within the infrastructure of his music...(This) album conveys sudden gleams of brilliance and thick and chunky hits, radio-friendly or not." *NME Magazine*, meanwhile, hailed the album as Tupac's "angry, end-of-tether, couldn't-give-a-shit meditation...An immense spewing of indignation and provocation, set to a brilliantly varied range of G-funk grooves...Tupac blasts out his non-PC opinions...with a competition-eliminating relentlessness."

The success of 'How Do You Want It' and therein, 'All Eyez on Me', gave Tupac and Johnny J the confidence and capital with Death Row to write their own ticket. As such, Johnny explained that, the combination of their success with 'All Eyez on Me', and the natural rate at which they outputted songs inevitably helped the producer feel as though "with me and Pac, it was almost like the more we worked, we could do this shit blind-folded. It was just amazing that the more you locked up and knocked songs out, it was just a natural chemistry that flowed out with no hesitation. So after we blew up with 'All Eyez on Me', it was on, such that Pac and I rarely ever left the studio. We'd stay in there till the break of dawn. All me and my wife would see was a recording studio and a bed at the Marriott Hotel. I kept my family with me in the studio because I was there so much. Maybe about 30 minutes at the mall to change into a fresh outfit, cause we had no time to go home, no time to do any outside activities. Because it was a consistent cycle—it was like this round-the-clock music factory that we kept going. We just kept going in this one mode, and me and Pac would work until I couldn't push buttons and he couldn't look at the microphone. We'd go 15, 18 hours straight in a day. There was an energy there, a feeling of this consistent creativity that just didn't want to stop. And there were alot of times when Pac would talk about death, and I know alot of fans have speculated on that and all, like 'He knew it was his time, that it was coming.' He wasn't like that in person, death was just one of so many subjects he touched on, the dude was just advanced. He had to think of everything you could think of, and he went into the death topic, and predicting his own death, 'I'm gonna get shot,' and he even said this to me: 'Johnny, when I die, you're gonna be trying to find me on a wegie board. I put that on everything.' And I was like 'Pac, what are you talking about?' And he was like 'You're gonna be going Tupac, where are you? I need you?'"

"He cracked a joke and said that to me. So when he was rapping about shot, it was more because it had been a part of his life, and anything else was theoretical pretty much. He knew he had been shot, and that it was a possibility that it could happen again, period. Straight up though, we did so many songs because he was so musically alive making them, not because he felt like his time was short. I would frame it that way, I would. The man was just so musically ahead of the game where that's where he had to go, that he went to the death subject, because he touched on stuff you wouldn't dare hear other people talk about or even try to discuss because it was too scary of a subject. Its kind of scary to just sit there and hear someone rap death, death, death, but Pac could put an authentic face on the subject because he'd come so close, so publicly. I felt as though he had to touch the subject just to let his fans know—spiritually—this is where I'd want to be if it did happen. This is what your gonna do—from my head to my toe—he's giving you basic instructions on what he wants done when he eventually leaves the earth. That's all he's saying. And he's just saying there's another side to things, another place besides this shitty ass earth that we live on man. Our sessions definitely had a timeless vibe to them, I don't know what it was, and I get this certain kind of spirit and vibe that I've dealt with in other people, but people would look at me and say 'There's something about you Johnny, that's very psychic. Things you say, the way and the way you do things in your music that gave you and Pac a lot in common.' A lot of things that Pac would touch on ended up happening."

While many within Tupac's inner-circle have suggested that Tupac completed 'All Eyez on Me' at such a rapid pace out of some hidden desire to quickly complete his contractual obligations to Death Row, or out of some sixth sense that his time on earth was short, Johnny felt Pac's real motivation to create at such a rapid pace was much less dramatic. For one, the producer felt that because Tupac, as a naturally proficient artist, having been locked down in a cell and out of the recording studio for almost a year, naturally had a lot of songs pent up he needed to get out of him and onto tape. Moreover, however, Johnny felt that much of what motivated the marathon sessions that became Tupac's signature at Death Row evolved naturally out of the music he and Johnny were creating together, such that "regarding the sheer amount of material that Pac produced during his time at Death Row, my whole vibe on the whole situation was that he was on such a good, consistent flow that that explains the proficiency."

"I know a lot of people do have that opinion of 'Well, he wanted to get all this music done and get off of Death Row.' And I can't confirm that, because I felt it was simply that the man had so much to say—especially coming off 9 months in prison of not being able to record anything, and that's like a lifetime for Pac creatively—that he had to do it in such a fast time frame because it was as though it just couldn't stop, his creative vibe. It was like this never-ending, ongoing creative mindstate he was in. He couldn't take a two-week break, we couldn't even get a week off from doing an album, because he couldn't just sit down and sit there and play a video game, and not get a song done. It was just something in him that kept him riding, and he'd say to me 'Johnny, I can't stay on this break period, I don't need a break.' I even remember him calling, and saying 'Johnny, we just finished *All Eyez On Me*, let's take a couple of weeks off.' So I was under this impression we were gonna take a nice little breather, but in all actuality, that probably lasted a day. We went right into the next song, and next song, and next song and carried on as though he could not stop. The spirits, and the creativity and the flow would not end. Where his mindstate was just on this vibe where he would say 'Johnny, I gotta keep going, something's telling me to keep going.' And when I look back at it now, that's the way I perceived it. You could just feel it in his attitude, it was as though 'Man, we gotta keep going till we can't do no more, till there's no more to come out of my brain.' Like we were gonna drain the hell out of our brains till we couldn't create. It was so advanced, and so ahead of our time and the game. Because I would translate lyrically what he wanted to say musically, for me that was my translation, I was saying it through the music. It was like a mirror. And he would say lyrically what I needed to be said on the music, for the whole thing to feel right and make sense. I knew where he was going. I just knew that anything that I would come up with—if it was the saddest track, or the most emotional track, or the most clubbish track—he was most motivational person I could ever be around, and I knew that anything I would create, he would know what subject and what concept to put to it. And I really respected and loved that about him, because I knew it was going to be a winner. It didn't have nothing to do with his popularity, or who he was, that he did movies, none of that. I didn't look a him as a celebrity, I looked at him as this advanced dude ready to get alot of shit off his chest."

As soon as Tupac got a topic off his chest, and Johnny got it onto tape, as the producer recalled, they passed the ball off to Death Row Records, who ran with it right into the streets. That the label could keep pace with Tupac and Johnny also allowed the duo to stay motivated because they didn't have to worry about a backlog of songs piling up, especially given Tupac's desire to flood the market with product, which mutually was Death Row's interest as well. As Johnny recalled it, one hand washed the other in an arrangement that kept Tupac happy and working, and kept the label bringing in enough revenues off of Tupac's record sales to justify the rapper dictating his own hours for studio occupation, usually 24-hour lockout—a freedom very few rap superstars enjoy unless they own their own recording facilities. Because Can Am Studios was an asset of the label, Tupac and Johnny were free to create without worrying about deadlines other than were natu-rally set by Shakur's own work ethic. In regard to the aforemen-tioned cycle, Johnny recalled that "one thing I can say about when Suge Knight had Death Row Records going, there was a man for every position. There was a guy who made sure that the half-inches got to Mastering, I made sure I was at mastering for 'All Eyez on Me.' So I was right there looking at everything from song 1 all the way to the last record. I think Death Row even had to make an adjustment when Pac first came on, because I don't think they expected such a rapid pace of music. It was just fast, so quick that we ran it like it was a factory. You couldn't keep me and Tupac out of the recording studio. So when Pac came to Death Row, it became like that was ours—at least in terms of Can Am, the studio they owned, because Tupac became the best seller overnight, and everyone made adjustments there to just let him do his thing in the Studio. Remember, that dude also fit in 9 videos, shot two motion pictures while he was at Death Row, so he just never stopped working. Their job at Death Row was just to try and keep pace with Pac—from the creation of the music to the retail release. They did a good job overall too. One thing I will also say for Suge is that there was never any pressure when we were recording from the outside. Like we never heard 'Oh my God, we're on an hourly rate.' Nothing like that, we were just flowing. Death Row definitely gave Tupac the freedom to work without the distractions of worrying about studio costs, or shit like that. That's a big fucking deal when you think about the fact that most studios rent out rooms at an 8-12 hour block, and you know if you don't get what you need to get done in that 8-12 hour block, the pressure gets on. The heat is on. And for me, it doesn't bother me because I'm quick at laying music, but some rappers, it can put alot of pressure on them. Pac wouldn't have given a fuck anyway, I wouldn't have either. We was notorious for going into overtime, even when we used to go to Echo Sound, before he got to Death Row."

Elaborating on the rarity of the arrangement for most producers and artists working in the industry, Johnny explained that "normally, if you only paid for 12 hours, and you ended up going into your 15th or 16th hour, you just did what you had to do. When we got to Death Row, Suge put the word out immediately that when Pac was in the studio, it was off limits—even between our sessions. We kept the big room at Can Am, the big room was me and Tupac's room always. We'd bounce back and forth between studio A and studio B, but all my equipment stayed in Studio A at all times. It was very well protected. When my stuff was set up and ready to go, it was very respected and well protected. Like the settings on the board, shit like that, no one touched anything. So once Pac and I were done for the night, that door was locked. Then the next morning, I'd walk back in and everything was exactly as we'd left it, still as is—including his Hennessey or whatever, everything was still the same. Then there were times when would *lock it down*. Lock-It-Down means we would make it where no one was to enter the studio unless it was of importance or you were to be on the record. So it got to a point where we'd gotten a little frustrated with all the traffic. We were on Death Row, so it got chaotic, with too many fucking spectators, riding off shit that we were doing. And there would be times where we were laying a song, and when I'd finished laying it, Pac and I would walk down the hall, and he'd be taking off for the night, and this was out at Can Am, Death Row's studio. So when I'd be walking back to the studio, I'd hear some of the same shit we'd just laid being mimicked in another studio, right down the hall. So I had to complain about that to Pac and Suge the next day, because I'd hear the concept of my bass line in another recording studio, and neither of them appreciated that shit at all, and had it cut out quickly."

"They ran a tight ship at Death Row, they kept the studio functioning, clean, it was a beautiful flow. There were rules there too, governing like—no one is to touch the equipment, or put their hands on anything Tupac and I had going on. If the 2-inch machine was still in the position it was in, it was not to be touched or tampered with. That was not to be tolerated. As relaxed as a recording studio is for the artist, you have to have rules and regulations for everyone else. I also personally loved the fact that when Tupac was on Death Row, it was a beautiful outlet because the records were instantly put out on the street, with no hesitation. When we recorded a record, in no more than a week's time frame—the record, as a single, was out, on sale at the record store. That was refreshing with the way Major Labels do thing, where putting out a record can be so time consuming—with release dates, and the corporate industry, being so slow, they need to wake up and learn how to put records out. Death Row definitely held up their end of the bargain on the release tip. One thing that was definitely open there, constantly flowing was studio time, at Death Row, and I'm not honestly sure another label could have offered Tupac that kind of freedom to record around the clock the way we were able to. It was never-ending, like the studio that never slowed down."

Of all the songs Johnny and Tupac recorded together during the 'All Eyez on Me' sessions, the favorite of he, Pac, and Suge was 'Life Goes On', which was anthematic of Tupac's personal philosophy for life. Elaborating on the making of the aforementioned tune, Johnny J recalled wistfully that "that's my favorite song I did with Tupac. That song had us in tears, we literally cried. At the time, I had the beat created way before I ever met Pac. There were beats that I had had for 4 or 5 years inside my vault, and I kept all these beats on standby, because in the time leading up to my collaboration with Pac, I never had artists who could meet the caliber of my music. So I felt like 'I don't want to give this to just any rap artist or singer who was going to fuck my shit off.' Its just gonna be a nice track, but the listener's not gonna like the lyrics or singer. And there was just something about that song when I laid it down, I loved Gamble and Huff, the Sounds of Philadelphia, I loved all the old O'Jays stuff. I loved every single record those guys produced, because I'm a Gamble & Huff fanatic, and I felt like I was a Gamble & Huff all in one, combined into a little Mexican package. So I just had to go with it, to where that song would water me up just as an instrumental, even before Pac even made up the lyrical concept for the song. So I started with the drum track, working my way into the bass synth, kind of tampering with the sample a little bit, so I kind of freaked it to add my flavor to it. Then layered those backgrounds on it, and that background vocal melody was in my head probably 3 to 4 years before I made it with Tupac, so I always had those backgrounds in my mind. I would actually sing that melody when me and my wife would listen to the instrumental in the car, house or whatever. And when the track finally got to Pac, I actually had 2 different singers sing two different sets of backgrounds. Usually, you don't combine two female vocalists—the way I did it—without an egotistical little vibe or something, where one is like 'What the hell is that, I'm supposed to be the only female on this record.' But I was like 'No, you sound beautiful, and you sound beautiful, so I'm gonna blend both of your chemistries into this song, so get up in the booth, and let's make it happen.' So in terms of my favorite Tupac records, I'll always go to 'Life Goes On', which puts me in a very emotional state. I don't break down in tears, but there's been times— throughout the years, and anniversary of his death—where I'll put that song on and it kind of breaks you down a little bit. But that song is very therapeutic for me, because it makes me think about how he was so excited about how the song turned out at the end—and how he was just very happy with the philosophy and overall concept of 'Life Goes On.' That whole memory of that evening will never leave my mind, it will be with me till the day I die. Pac's not here with me physically, but he is here, so I feel like he's with me wherever I go. I learned so much from him—that sometimes with things around you, you just gotta kind of go with the flow, and just gotta kind of accept it. I saw that in play from just being around him constantly, and we just kind of dealt with it together." As with many of the songs Tupac recorded during this period in his career, no one could have known the theme this song would become for his fans following his tragic passing a year later in helping both those who admired and personally knew and loved him to understand and move past his death in time.

Chapter 10
Timeless Tracks—Tupac and Johnny J

While Tupac's work ethic inspired the majority of Death Row's fellow artist roster to follow suit, it was often impossible to keep pace both because of Tupac's natural talent, but also because the Death Row world naturally revolved around Tupac as the label's chief money maker. It was simply a matter of dollars and sense as Johnny J saw it, such that "there were definitely artists on Death Row who were like 'Oh shit, we better get in the lab, because Tupac and Johnny J are dishing out too many hits. We better get our ass on our P's and Q's. Tupac is in here smashing, so we better get our shit together too.' I felt as though Tupac and I, we set examples for Death Row. We even opened up new ways of saying 'Get up off your lazy ass and get some work done.' I think Pac and my work ethic motivated all the Death Row artists, including Snoop, Danny Boy, everyone who was there. I thought it elevated their model." While Tupac generally kept one of the main studios in Can Am on 24-hour lockdown for his sessions, he was also extremely generous to his fellow Death Row artists, the Outlawz, and to his family, who were usually the only non-artist related audience he allowed to be present during sessions.

As Johnny J recalled in particular, Tupac always enjoyed when his mother was present at the studio, explaining that in one such situation, "Afeni was in the studio when we were recording 'Picture Me Rolling.' Afeni was a proud mom, looking at her son blossoming, doing what he does. He loved to have her in there watching while he was recording, it was real motivational for him. I remember at the time—tracking that song—as well as some others we did while she was in the studio, that it was a real cool motivation for Pac, you could just feel the glow, and the spirit going on. It was almost like a reunion for him, almost like there was a cleansed spirit in the air between him and his mom at the time. It was really really cool, a very spiritual vibe. And his family, at the time, showed me a great deal of appreciation for what I was doing for their son. She looked like 'Man, this Mexican kid is bringing some real music to my son's lyrics.' She kept a smile on her face, and just let Pac do his thing. Never tried to chime in, she left it as is, and had the respect not to even comment, not to interfere. Was never like 'Baby I don't like that,' or 'You know better than that.' She didn't interfere with any of the songs we did at all, just kept a glowing smile on her face and loved and enjoyed it. It was just a big party, one of the big celebrations we had, whenever Afeni was in the studio with us. It was like a barbecue, and it was funny, because after we'd finish certain songs when Afeni and Pac's sister, and other family was around, we'd take the party from the studio straight over to my house, and my wife and I would host barbecues. Tupac, the Outlawz, his family, it was nice. It was like one big family."

Topically, the subject matter of Tupac's songs depended not on his audience but rather on his mood in the moment. As such, Johnny J recalled that Shakur could also record on any number of varied, topically-opposite subjects in a given recording session, over the course of 4 or 5 songs, or inside of just one, over the course of as many verses. For the producer, Tupac was the most lyrically diverse rapper he ever worked with, and therein, the most talented, such that "we could go from a sexual record, which could be the funniest thing, with a club beat, where he could be talking about 'partying and dancing, and I wanna get my freak on', and then jump into the next track and be like 'I don't know what it is

Johnny, but I need to talk about Mama's just a little girl. Something took me there.' And to just jump from that to that, or the other way around, to go in the same session from the saddest record to the most clubbed-out record, we touched every ground and level you could think of. We never had a pattern of 'We need to do two club songs, then two sad songs. Or we need to do an up, a mid and a slow.' There was never a pattern, it was whatever was going through his head at the time. I would just adapt musically with him. I noticed when he got quiet, when he would get into this quiet state, and kind of bite his lip, you could tell we were getting ready to go into a sad mode. You could feel we were getting ready to do an emotional record or a very touching song. And it didn't necessarily need to be some sad song where we were all going to be in tears, but I knew he was gonna do a slow track. Where we were gonna do something real mellow and pretty. I loved him for the fact that I could do a pretty beat—a very beautifully produced track—and he could also do an aggressive vocal on it. I'll give you a good example—'U Wonder Why They Call You Bitch.' If you listen to the record thoroughly, it's kind of sad what he's explaining, it was a sad topical song with a club beat under it at the same time. And he was also relaying a message to the women 'You wonder why they call you bitch? You're out there spreading yourself around, giving yourself up, opening your legs to anything that walks in.' You gotta analyze that shit, and say its a prostitute or a girl at a club—and there's millions of them— women that just open their legs to any given thing that walk in. And for women to listen to something like that, that's gotta hit home. To me, the track was clubby, and the subject matter was so mixed up between political and personal levels, that it was real…"

"Another like that was 'Shorty Wanna Be A Thug.' It was kinda smooth that day, a laid-back session. Pac started thinking about how these kids think. He was like, 'Little homies just want to be a thug.' He just put that title up there, and the subject just jumped off. It gave Napoleon a vibe of making him think it was about him. I kinda looked at it the same way. It was as if he was talking about Napoleon. He saw his parents murdered in front of him. Napoleon had a hard upbringing. He was going through it. It was like a therapeutic vibe. It had Tupac thinking for a minute…The emotional songs were his favorite. Then there was times when we did songs, where he would have what we'll call an 'angry' vocal style, where there was a more aggressive sound to it, and it would work. It was just a way of him getting his point across, and I would say his background as an actor definitely informed the mood of his vocals, but the sincerity and authenticity was always there naturally. His acting ability and theatrical skills definitely brought alot to the table, because he could sit there—with any song—and picture it like it was this movie that you could see from beginning to end. Its so beautiful the way he would do it, because he would theme out like the most critical story you could ever think of. His stories would consist of how he woke up that morning, what he ate, who he talked to, who he saw get beat up in the street, who he saw at the red light, and then he would come to the studio and turn that into a magical record. It was definitely art imitating life with Pac. That motherfucker could talk about Chicken Wings or women's rights and it didn't matter, he always brought the appropriate mood to the subject matter he was rapping on in his style of delivery, tone, intensity, all of that."

Any in-depth examination of Tupac's harder material should center on the making of 'Hit 'Em Up', historically regarded as the most venomous battle rap in the genre's history. As Johnny J recalled Tupac's attitude toward his angrier-toned, shit-talking rally raps, "sincerity was a general theme with Pac on any song he rapped on, topically. He was always in the moment. You have to remember too, we have what we call the West Coast. And in my production style, I represent both coasts, and for that reason, alot of people call my music timeless. Someone said to me once 'You have what I'd call forever music, because it lasts forever. It never dies out.' Well, Pac was that way too, that's why we cliqued so well, but obviously what he rapped lyrically over my music defined the song. So if it was a harder track, obviously I would be giving him rougher music to rap over. We built most of those harder tracks on the spot in the studio. And you have to remember, Pac was trying to keep the West Coast sound on deck. Pac had this thing when he got to Death Row, like as a theme, where he said 'Come on man, we gotta bring this shit up to the next level.' And so when he said things in songs that might have taken the beef to another level, he was just trying to keep the coast up, he was trying to keep the West Coast on the map. And that shit truly rested on his shoulders too, because to me, ever since he's been gone, the West Coast has been fucked up. He was the pinnacle of that sound. And there was a very deep authenticity to those songs."

Regarding 'Hit 'Em Up' specifically, which Tupac wrote at the studio at the height of the East Coast-West Coast beef between he and Biggie, Johnny recalled that the hatred on the record heard in Tupac's voice and words toward Biggie and the East Coast at large was 100% authentic. According to the producer, while the track was more personal based on the beef between he and Biggie, that Shakur could in the same time take on the entire East Coast rap scene based on the adrenaline he had pumping in his veins, the vibe was almost super-human, such that "that had to be the most hard core record I've ever done in my career, I haven't topped that shit yet. I don't even plan on doing any more records like that. I've made this deal—based on the impact of that song—that I don't want to do records going against any coast, or based on gang members going against each other, Bloods or Crips. I just don't want anything like that recorded again. I mean, we made history, I love the record, don't get me wrong, I'm very happy with the work I put in on it. The lyrics are a mother fucker though! It was a very angry rapper in the studio that night, Pac was upset. One of the angriest vocals I've ever done with him. When Pac is angry like that naturally, like before he step in the booth, you better leave him that way going into the session. Because one thing about Pac was that when he would get upset on that level—and there are other records I did with him where he would get this anger in him, where it would just pour out on the vocals, even on like 'Little Homies.' But you gotta just let him go, its like a boxer in the ring. Don't fuck with him, just let him flow. He may have been an actor, and people might have thought he was acting out an angry part or whatever on some of his shit—not on that song, 'Hit 'Em Up.' That shit was true feelings, true attitude—everything in the record that you hear vocally was from the fucking heart. You can't get any more authentic than that, because the man didn't have to front and lie."

"It was funny on 'Hit 'Em Up' too because, with the way Pac recorded his vocal tracks, he would get angrier and angrier with every vocal track he laid. He took that shit to another level of anger. Because when you got to the double, after he'd already completed the first lead vocal track, when he got to the double, and triple, and fourth tracks, he had gotten angrier and angrier. So that process actually amplified the intensity of Pac's vocal to the next highest level you can think of, to where his fucking voice was going out. He would do that shit so much at times that he would literally throw his vocals out, where his voice would completely go out. He'd usually be out a day, or a blunt and some Hennessey would bring it back. And it was good for him to have the day's break after we recorded 'Hit Em Up' because his voice actually went out at the end. And especially after completing a record like that, he needed a breather, probably a day or a day and a half. So it was therapeutic at times when his voice would blow. Because of the venting, the shit he had to get off his chest in the studio."

Given Tupac's usual desire in any given session to record continuously, Johnny for his part was grateful for the break the song dictated the rapper take, as it gave his producer more time to mix, which was perhaps the only part of the recording process Johnny preferred Tupac be gone for. A producer always puts in longer hours than his artist, usually in much greater measure, but Tupac was unique in that he usually kept pace with Johnny J for the duo's average 15-17 hour sessions. Still, to hear his producer tell it in hindsight, while he worked quickly when mixing, Johnny almost always preferred that Tupac be gone, explaining that "in the mix process, Pac could not hang around for mixing, he would always leave. And I used to love it when he would leave, I would celebrate. And I'm gonna tell you why: we would track our asses off. Say we'd tracked three songs in a day—which was usually our average—I've done the tracks, music's done, lyrics are done, the hook is done. So we'd get all that over with, and it would usually be a good 3 to 4 cuts, and I'd look at him and go 'Please leave so I can start mixing.' Because if I was mixing, he would actually walk back into the studio, while I was working, and go 'J, I know you're mixing, but I want to cut another song. I got a vibe. I got another title for you. I got a concept.' And it used to piss me off because I'd go 'I'm trying to mix man.' And literally I'd have to stop what I was doing and address it, and it wouldn't mean a damn thing, because if Pac wanted to record, we were recording. And if he was there, he'd always go 'I know your trying to mix Johnny, but we gotta do another song.' And I'd be like…'You dickhead.' And he'd just look at me like 'Yep, let's do another one.'"

"We had a lot of jokes like that between us, but he was always serious about interrupting me to record a new song. My approach to mixing was structured pretty much the same for all my artists, I didn't treat anyone very differently. It just happened that I did alot more specific work with Pac, so we had our formula down. I have the easiest mixes you could ever imagine because they didn't take 8 to 9 hours, really because they couldn't with the number of songs we was pumping out of each session. I mean, some time-bandit producers that you have out there in the game take 2 to 3 days to mix one song. You got to be out your fucking mind to take that kind of time to mix one song. Usually my rough mixes are pretty close to what you hear on the actual album, so when I transitioned from tracking to mixing, there really wasn't that much to change.

In fact, some of the final mixes you hear are really rough mixes. I didn't even do a final mix, because they were so beautifully leveled, had the roughness I needed, I didn't need to EQ too much shit but here and there, didn't need to polish up too much stuff, because when you did it took the grittiness away. So I kept it gritty, by leaving the mix in the moment of the way we were tracking—whether everyone was tipsy, or partying, or whatever—that was pretty much the mix. We would do our little fine tuning, adjust the vocals, put whatever effects we had to put on them to enhance them or bring them out, but that was actually how I would mix. I would mix a song in a good 3 to 4 hours, maximum 5 hours per track."

Chapter 11
Non-Stop Productions—Tupac and Johnny J

As the months wore in into later 1995, Tupac and Johnny's pace continued to expand with the average of 15 songs a week they would turn into Death Row, eventually reaching a point— both professionally and personally—where they felt a catalog was developing. Without any concept of how important that work would become to defining Tupac's legacy in the long term, Johnny recalled that as friends, a comfort level had developed which allowed that, for his part as a producer, "I was never intimidated by Pac working with other producers, never got like 'Oh, that's fucked up, you let them step onto my little world here, you let another producer in.' I was never intimidated by that, because I knew I was the shit at the time. I knew I was fading their asses, knew they couldn't fuck with me. So basically, I was pretty God-damn arrogant, because I was just very confident of my work, so any other outside producer, I'm not gonna front. It never really intimidated me whatsoever, I was open to the idea because I loved the fact that my recorded ended up being the ones that shined the most anyway, so it all worked out beautifully. When Pac and I would hand in a new batch of what was usually 4 or 5 songs from a given day's recording session, and once the mixes were completed."

Elaborating on the underpinnings of his confidence in why he and Tupac's creative flow could not be interrupted, Johnny identifies the fact that "On an intellectual level, we really connected to where I learned from him, and felt as though, deep in his heart, he learned from me. I think, in a certain sense, he looked at the relationship between me and my wife, and our kids, who were in the recording studio every time I worked on a track with him, I have studio babies. They grew up there. And my wife is my business partner, I kind of felt he looked at that and felt like 'Man, I wanna be like that. I wanna feel that family vibe, I want that wife and the kids, one day I'm gonna feel that.' I even got that kind of feedback from him, where some days he'd be like 'Damn man, the family life.' You could just see it in his eyes that he wanted it. He truly loved kids, loved the hell out of kids, would constantly grab my daughter, always embracing kids. My daughter was around 2, and my son was around 4 or 5. And with the kids around, we knew when to say things a certain way, or when not to, but as far as cussing or whatnot, it really didn't matter too much. We were realistic about what we were talking about, we were raised on 'Fuck' and words like that, and we wouldn't get too raunchy or raw with it, but he and I were so close that that I guess I trusted him as much as he trusted me not to trip. We both felt like 'Hey, this is the real world, and we're not gonna lie to them. They gonna hear what's going on. Lets not sugarcoat none of the shit we're doing.' And it was probably a good kind of insurance with all of his music, because he always kept it so real, but to be as raw as he was with my kids around, you know he kept it real."

Continuing, Johnny regarded the most enjoyable element of his collaboration with Tupac as "his natural vibe, the natural human being that he was—the kindest, the coolest comedian ever. We were comedians together, we cracked jokes on each other non-stop, that I truly miss about him. That other side of him, that people never really got to see. People perceived him to be this thug, or gangster and bad guy, I still get that kind of shit even to this day. Truthfully, they didn't know who Pac was, he was truthfully a really beautiful man. A really good guy, the nicest guy I could ever have worked with, the greatest rapper I've ever worked with in my life. No one's ever gonna get better than that. To just sit there and just hear the track, and just come off the head and right into that pad, from the pencil to the paper, and just to see the shit just written for every song right there in front of my face. I'd always be sitting there, right to the left of him, just looking over there. This is what he did, how he wrote: I'd play him a beat, and then after he'd get done with his first verse, he'd pull me over to the side, and recite it to me in my ear, and pretty much get my approval, what I thought. And I'd be like 'Man, you get your ass in the vocal booth and handle that. You don't need my approval.' But it was a respect thing, that he sought it because he trusted me, I love how he did that. One thing I always loved about the way he'd write: the shit made sense, and what he wrote about, it all came together. He could write about 60 different things in one verse. There's not too many rap artists, at least among those I've worked with, who could ever do shit like that. It could be a damn club record, like 'How Do You Want It', and he could talk about everything from sex to politics and fit it all into one record. I love how he'd combine all those fucking elements. The tone of his voice, he just had this magical tone that fucked me up every time I heard it. I loved that shit. I also loved the fact whatever drum pattern I had, whatever musical rhythmic pattern I had going on in a song, he could follow that same pattern lyrically, and actually match the way I patterned the kick vocally. So vocally it would be the same, identical way. I felt like that was his appreciation to me, saying 'I love your music so much, that I'm gonna follow your lead. I'm gonna follow what you did creatively lyrically. I'm gonna do it lyrically the way you did your kick or your bassline.' I miss that about him. Pac had a really cool, confident attitude about himself—if you want to call him arrogant, it was an arrogance that sold records man. But overall, he was a pretty humble dude."

The level of trust and mutual respect that Tupac and Johnny had built between them over the course of the dozens of songs they had recorded together by this point also allowed the pair to openly learn from one another in boundless ways that continually informed both their writing and recording process, such that, as Johnny recalled it, "Pac and I definitely learned from each other all the time—the one thing I will never forget that I taught him was how to mute out elements. Its called how to arrange a record. He'd never worked a board, never used the cut button, or the mute button. But I was always using them, and when he'd be partying to it after the song was lyrically completed, I would be sitting there playing with the mute buttons, giving it kind of a live, on the spot, spontaneous arrangement. And he would look over at me, and go 'Oh shit, teach me that Johnny.' And I showed him, and there were times when I regretted showing him because he got a little too happy with the shit. He was a very quick learner, and he loved to mute out bass lines, and bring the Rhodes in, and bring the guitar in. Whatever the musical instrument was at the time, it was just a fun thing to do. And sometimes we would work the board together as a team, with him on the right and me on the left, and we're just looking at each other vibing, like 'Let's push a mute here, let's drop it all out, and bring it on back.' It was a real good party vibe. It was open minded at all times when we were producing, and in general when I was producing Pac. Say, for instance, I made up with a nice keyboard or mood line, a real beautiful mood line, or something real catchy on a rugged, street level, he'd follow my lead. He'd go off of me, and go 'Oh, okay, J put down that nice keyboard line down, let me vibe with him.' Then it would work sometimes visa versa, where I would vibe with him, I would listen to actual way he would form the melody or structure out a different melodic pattern in his vocals, so when he would leave and I would go into a mix mode. I would think to myself, 'Let me do a little keyboard line under the melody he just created, and structure it a little differently, put a little different layer on it.' It was like making a cake, with the cherry at the top. It was just beautiful man."

Further, the relationship that Tupac and Johnny shared personally, coupled with their natural professional chemistry, allowed for a much more naked environment in the studio, wherein there were no holds barred on what could be said on tape, and no boundaries on where the duo could push their sound as a result. The trust they placed in each others hands with their music before any of it would ever reach those of the fans allowed that when it did, Tupac's record buyers were virtually guaranteed to be both satisfied on a basic listening level, but also challenged to possibly see things in a different light given the places Tupac was taking them lyrically. The foundation for that freedom on the listener's part to expand his own perspective's horizons rooted in what Johnny J described as "open honesty in the studio. Pac and my key thing in the studio with anyone was open honest, where we don't have no problems with saying what we have to say. Either your ass is gonna bring it, or we're gonna let you know your shit is garbage. I have a very direct approach about the way I produce people, about the way I even coach vocals. Because I'll let them know 'That shit you just sang is horrible. And I don't really appreciate the shit the way you just sang it.' And I kind of use that attitude to motivate, and it does work as a motivational piece because I don't give a fuck about the crying—if she's a female singer and she starts getting sensitive, that shit's for the birds. It does not matter if she's a no name or a star, I've worked with Ron Isley all the way down the line, and I don't talk shit and disrespect, or anything like that. But I don't treat them any different than who the new person is, whether they been around 50 years or they're brand new to the game. And I love Ron Isley for the fact of even having the decency to ask me when I was recording him, 'Johnny, am I doing it right? Am I doing my vocals the way they need to go?' I really looked at that as an honor. That's when I did 'Better Days', but I said to him 'Ron, you're doing beautiful, but you could go back and do this again, and do that again.' And with no hesitation, the man had the respect to say 'No problem, let's go back and do it again.' But my key thing with everyone is that I don't kiss ass. I don't care who it is. It doesn't matter who you are, you have to be up front and frank about shit because sugar-coating things and speaking soft on it is corny bullshit. If your shit doesn't sound good on my record, I'm gonna tell you I don't like it. Period."

As Johnny explained it, while he and Pac rarely ever crossed into that territory personally, it felt good to be have that air of freedom as creative oxygen. For Tupac and Johnny, it was more of a license to laugh at that rare, late-night track that should have been aborted long before it was ever born. Still, at the rate he and Pac were birthing new music, according to Johnny, one particular song came out with the litter that both felt should never have seen the light of day. As the producer remembers, "Tupac and I really didn't have that problem, but it was open air always in case we needed to. He and I never really had any discrepancies about any songs though, never had an argument about a record. There was only one song we did together that we both hated—we hated the SHIT out of it. Its called 'Fair Exchange', and let me tell you, nobody knows this story. That was the song Tupac and I did not like—and it was originally done a different way—but we hated the record together when it was recorded. We honestly looked at each other, and Pac said 'Do you know that shit was wack as hell?!' And I looked at him and said 'Pac, you're ass is wack too!' So we both got to look at each other, and say 'That was a fucked-up record we did.' I know lyrically, if you listen to it now, its probably not as bad as you think, but back when we recorded it, that song we hated together. It was a forced issue, we had another guy sing the hook that was garbage, it was pure trash. And we were up there letting the guy sing the hook, like we accepted it like it was great. We were so tired by that point in the day, that we were both very passive, like 'Yeah, that came out good.' Knowing fucking well it was horrible. I think that was the shittiest fucking session we ever had, because we worked up till 4 or 5 in the morning, and it was one of those 'late-nighters'. And I knew it was either that we were too exhausted, and tried to drink a little Hennessey with it, and the shit didn't mix, and it showed on our creativity that night. I was pretty happy with the rest of the songs we did."

In fact, shortly before his tragic passing in October of 1996, Johnny J and Tupac had accumulated such a back catalog of material—approximately 150 songs—that they had reached a point where were almost rap-wearied. As such, the duo had made plans to move above and beyond the ceiling of hip hop, planning to cross-over into the neighboring musical genres as songwriters and producers. As Johnny J described their plans, "the production Pac and I formed at the time we were working together after he got out of prison was called 'Non-Stop Productions.' It was a vibe where he asked me personally, 'I want you to create a name for us to do our own thing. Johnny, I want to be the one who writes the lyrics, you do the music, and we're gonna be like L.A. and Babyface.' This was for future artists that he had plans and intentions on working with—Mary J. Blige, Alanis Morrissette, you name it. These were artists he was just musically infatuated with. And I loved him for the fact that he loved to go to those levels of music. Pac was also a Prince fanatic, we all are. We were so honored that—at the time—when we wanted to use anything Prince had to clear—it was a cleared thing, the sample was cleared. I loved it, I can respect Prince for that, and for respecting Pac. Even when we used the sample for '777-9311', that was originally a Time track that Prince had written, and produced—by Jamie Starr, who was Prince. So no matter who the artist was, whenever Pac and I collaborated, we had a thing where he would come into the studio with a CD in his hand, after listening to it in his car, and he'd always say 'Johnny J, I got one for you!' And I'd say 'What?' And he'd pop an oldie in, an old classic cut, and go 'What you think?' And I'd go 'Let's put it down.' So I'd do my thing with my sampler, and then put my musical elements around it, and it would turn into this magical chemistry. Say for instance he brought in a certain CD, and he always called me Captain Kirk, and he'd play me the sample he liked, and then say 'Put your Star trek Enterprise shit on it, and we know what we're doing here.' He also called me Tito Puentez too, because of my Latin roots."

Big Syke further testified to Tupac's talent as a co-producer, recalling that for the recording of the track 'What's Ya Phone #', based on the Prince sample '777-9311', "Pac was a tight producer too. Think about that Prince beat he flowed over, his flow on that shit was just tight. He picked that beat, and had Johnny J flip it a certain way. That's what was dope, he'd tell Johnny 'Grab this beat, flip this.' He was constantly telling Johnny 'Flip this.' Most of the time, Johnny J would bring up a beat he had already pre-programmed in the machine, but some beats, that 'Time' album beat that Prince produced under Jamie Starr. When Johnny first did it, he did it on the one, it wasn't the same tempo, it was off. So Pac had him put it back the way the beat originally sound. How the drums is, Johnny looped it a different way, but then Pac said 'Naw, do it how the beat was before.' Cause the way Johnny had looped it, it wasn't the same drum pattern, it was off tempo. So Pac flipped the fuck out that shit." Continuing his praise, Johnny J remembered that "Pac had no limitation to his musical tastes, everything was acceptable—it could be a record from the 40s, and we'd turn it into a hit. Pac had a whole lot more to say, and I knew it was about to be on and cracking with what we were planning. I knew it was about to be this enterprise, this corporate level of non-stop music. That's why we named our company Non-Stop Productions, because it was literally this non-stop music machine. We were very intimidating, even at Death Row Records, because we were creating music at such a rapid pace. There were people that just couldn't maintain the rate at which we were dishing out our music, because we were doing it so fast and so creatively, that it broke with the mold. Because it didn't take us 12, 13 14 hours to create one damn song. With what Pac and I would do in 14 hours, we were walking out of there with 4 or 5 completed records ready to go be mixed. So we were on a serious mission. We had alot more hit records to make." Sadly, the pair would never get the chance.

September 7, 1996:
The Day the Music Died...

When Tupac was murdered on September 7, 1996, Johnny J, the man who had spent the most singular and concentrated creative time in the studio with Tupac over the last period of his life, was "personally and artistically devastated. It was like my other half is gone again. It was like being hit with the impact of when he went to jail. I was like 'Oh no, not again man.' Creatively, I still had the most creative shit musically on my mind; it's just that when he left, I just wasn't motivated to create at the time. At that time, I wasn't happy with the artists I was hearing and trying to work with, because it was just unacceptable, not up to my level. I felt like I was forcing the issue, so I decided to put the producing on hold—which is not to say I retired, or wanted to stop producing records—I just wanted to kind of hold up a minute. To evaluate everything, and see where things were going. It didn't affect my creativity in the long run, but Pac's passing was just a drastic hit, a real deep, critical situation. I just had a real serious break-down. I had arrived in Vegas like 15 minutes before he actually died, and was on the way to meet him. Me, my wife, Big Skye, and quite a few other friends got to Las Vegas, and all got the news together. And it was like losing a big part of me, because I felt like I was left alone in the music industry. I felt like it was all me again, because he's not here. He was there in spirit, and our music is here to live and stay and go on forever. But personally, it was like I was back to the instrumentals, so it took me a while to bounce back. I felt really obligated to him; because I was always open to working with other artists, but most of what came my way after he died was shit that didn't make any sense for me to record. I feel like there were so many more levels that I wanted to take it to with Pac, and when he passed, it was like I had to start over. I'm not saying in career-aspects, but I just felt like I was starting over. Pac's always gonna be a part of me—no matter who I produce, no matter what I work on, no matter where I go in life. He's always there with me in spirit. He's part of my foundation for everything—part of my everyday routine. Me and my wife and kids—his spirit is even here with my family. But artistically—and personally—after that day, a part of me died with him I think. Today, I use that emptiness to motivate myself creatively, because I know there is more that's written for me, before I close the chapters. That's what Pac would have wanted. I just wanna keep going."

The rest of the world suffered the loss as personally in their own individual ways—from listeners, to business associates, to friends, to fans, to family, and on and on. It could be argued that the world might not have healed from the deficit hip hop faced with Tupac's death had it not had the massive catalog of unreleased music he recorded during his lifetime to fill the void. Beginning with 'Makaveli: The Don Killuminati: The 7 Day Theory', recorded in the final months of Tupac's life and arguably his deepest contribution in teachings to the movement he had founded and led throughout his wondrous career. Inarguably the most intellectually enlightened and spiritually prophetic hip-hop album ever recorded and released commercially, *Rolling Stone Magazine's* review of the record shortly following Tupac's death hailing its 14 tracks as "fat with funky menace…and the choral-vocal effect in many of the raps has a street-corner, pass-the-bottle charge." Recalling the overall vibe of the album's creation, musician and engineer Darryl Harper recalled that "the album was finished in three days, (and) the mixing still had to be done. So the album was done in a week. As for Pac's parts, all of them was done in 3 days...He would have ideas for it, he would know. He would instantly tell the Outlawz to what they needed to be writing about. And they had to be on it, because the one that didn't have it, he wasn't going to be on that song. It was a trip because Pac would finish his vocal, come out (from the booth) and point at one of them. If he stuttered, he would point to the next one. He just missed that track. If they weren't confident right away, he would let them know they weren't going to be on there." Producer Hurt M. Badd, who collaborated with Shakur on tracks for the album, recalled that the rapper's pace for the Makaveli sessions were vintage Tupac, wherein the album's 12 tracks were recorded in 7 days. As the producer recalled, "Pac had just finished his album 'All Eyes on Me' so his next album he was like, 'I want to get this done real quick.' So I was already into making tracks and doing them quick...(Pac always recorded) quick, fast and in a hurry...He was just like, 'I gotta get this done, I can't let nothing stop me. I gotta get it done and get it done now.' ...I work fast, so it was like right up my alley...(but I think all the album's producers) seemed to take to everything and be on time as well." Continuing, Hurt M. Badd explains that his collaboration with Tupac—albeit brief—was still lasting in that he learned from "the way (Pac) worked real quick, the way he took things so serious. He knew what he could do and he just got in there and did it. That rubbed off on me as well...(When we did 'Hail Mary', it) only took me 15, 20 minutes to create the whole beat. I just came to work one day, I was feeling good. I was sitting behind the boards. I just touched a few sounds man, and it was like done. And so an engineer came into the room where I worked, and he heard the track—I told him to put the headphones on. He looked at me like 'Damn Hurt, that sounds like a funeral, man.' When I do stuff, I don't be feeling it like everybody else, I guess cause its me. He said 'Why don't you let Tupac hear this?' When Tupac heard it, he didn't really say nothing but 'Gimmie that.' I left the studio and when I came back the next day, everybody from the security guard to the phone lady to the engineer—everybody ran up to me like 'Wait to you hear what this nigga done laid over your track.' When I heard it, I didn't think it was a hit. I was like 'Why is Tupac laying this stuff over my track?' We all had a listening party for the album, and Pac was loving every song, but when they played that song, he just went through a thing. He threw his hand up with his Hennessey bottle, he threw his hand up like he ruled a nation."

Engineer Lance Pierre, who mixed the hit, recalled for his part that "that was the best song on the record. It was also the strangest song. What I mean by that is the way it came out at the end as far as 'Makaveli the Don' and all that. Tupac used to do a lot of that ad-lib. Just talking toward the end of the song. I was mixing it, and none of that shit was supposed to come out like that. But it came out and it sounds good. I'm talking about the outro, where you hear 'Makaveli the Don.' That was some extra stuff. That was a total fluke. The song is supposed to stop there. But it sounded good, so we just kept it and turned it into an interlude with the whole monk thing going on. That one turned out more than really how we expected it to work out." Producer Darryl Harper recalled during the making of the album's opening tune, 'Bomb First', that "I presented the beat to Pac and he liked it, but he wanted the bass line changed. He wanted the bass line similar to the one someone had done on the movie Juice, (Naughty by Nature's 'Uptown Anthem.) I didn't know what it was like, so I had to get it and find out what it was like. So I changed the bass line and it went like that." Engineer Lance Pierre elaborated on the latter, explaining that "Tupac actually did that bass line. He actually sat up on the Moog and punched out each button on that. But Darryl did the beat. Pac did the song; a lot of people don't know that it seemed like Pac was getting off into production. That was one of the songs that Tupac had a lot to do with as far as the production of it." Recalling the creation of another hit from the album, 'To Live and Die in L.A.', producer QDIII recalled that "I was in the studio with Pac, I had some records with me, and there was this old song that I played for him to see if he liked the vibe. He felt it and told me to go home and hook up a beat like that. I went home and hooked it up as fast as I could, and I think I came back the same night and he listened to the track three times. In like 15 minutes he was already done with the lyrics. He went into the booth without telling anyone what the track was about, and he just laid it in one take—over about three tracks. Then he told Val Young what the concept was, and she went in and laid the chorus vocal in one take—too. After the vocals were done, Pac had Ricky Rouse replace my keyboard bass and guitar parts with live bass and guitar parts, and the song was done—less than two hours total. That song just flowed out of everyone who was a part of it. No one thought twice, no one doubted anything. It was full speed ahead till it was done—as if it was guided or meant to be. Ever since recording like that, without thinking twice like that, I have changed the way I look at making music." On the track 'Krazy', engineer Lance Pierre remembered that "the song wasn't really put together, it was just a beat. Kevin Lewis (jazz pianist Ramsey Lewis' cousin), who was actually the project coordinator, he was there and we kept saying 'Man, this is not a song.' He said 'But Tupac wants that song on the record.' I said, 'Man, I got it mixed, but its still not sounding right.' He said 'It just needs some piano.' So he just went in there and just played according to the vocals. The song turned out a lot better that it originally was."

On the track 'White Man'z World', engineer Darryl Harper recalled that "Pac wrote the hook. I had did a beat; he liked it. He wrote the melody and everything for the hook and I sung it." Producer Hurt M Badd further remembered that for the creation of tracks 'Me and My Girlfriend', 'Hold Ya Head', and 'Against All Odds', "on 'Girlfriend', he tried to bluff me, he called me out. After we had done like 4 songs, Tupac had called me in my session and one day—now mind you, I work in my own little production room. Tupac called me in his room one day and he said 'You know what? I need a kind of up-tempo beat that don't sound like

125

anything you ever done before.' So my eyebrows raised and I was like 'Whoa.' So he said 'And I want you to stand right here and create it right in my face.' Let me tell you something.' Everything surrounding my heart went to my feet. Sweat just broke out all under my arm. But I'm also that type of person, I love a challenge when it comes to something I do…So Tupac said 'Right now, in my face.' So I started from scratch. I just told the DJ to sample a kick and a snap from the keyboard. Everybody was looking at me like 'What?' Looking at me crazy like 'He don't know what he's doing.' Before you know it, I had the drums going, and I look over at the guy with the bass guitar. I told him to come in with something, and I gave him a little rhythm. He came in with it. Before you know it, Tupac was on the couch—he had this look on his face like 'I don't believe this guy!' By the time we laid the guitar strings, he was up on the floor like 'Yeah.' Every time he'd get a track he liked, he would listen to it and come up with the hook in his head…(For 'Hold Ya Head'), Pac did the verse and the hook already. He came in my room and asked me if I knew how to sing. He said he wanted me to sing on the hook. I said, 'I'll be right in there.' When he shut the door, I just started jumping up and down in a room by myself. When I went in there, I got real nervous. He gave me the notes to sing and everything. And fortunately, it turned out cool. Anytime you had to rap or sing with him, that's how he was, (he expected you to work fast…On 'Against All Odds'), he was getting his weapons for war, his arsenal ready. The day we made that song Tupac said 'I need a war song. I wanna go to war.' He gave me an hour and then came back and heard the beat, and he wanted me to add that Cameo song bassline. Once it was in, Pac started snapping, 'This is it.' He called the Outlawz in and started reciting the hook, 'This be the realest shit I ever wrote.' While Pac was doing his vocals, he wasn't just recording his vocals, he was also kicking over the music stand, hitting the microphone. There was a vibe in the room."

Outlawz member and Tupac protégé Napolian recalled the vibe of the Makaveli recording sessions as one in which "he was on a whole other mission. When he wrote that song about Blasphemy, I remember him saying 'Man, I don't even remember how I got that stuff.' He was saying quotes from the bible, but then I remember him saying 'I don't remember how it all just flowed out of my mouth like this.' It was a deep record. That's what I saw him going through, and its like he put it out in the music. I think, being around Pac and the way he was talking, I think he knew his time was up, he felt he could have died at any minute. Pac showed that so much man, especially right before he passed away. He got a camera, he used to buy is little portable cameras, and would say 'I want y'all to go around and snap pictures.' Even when he fought the dude in Vegas, soon as he fought the dude, I was in California, and he called me that night after the fight. 'Call moo.' And I missed the call. I really feel he felt that was coming, which is why he did so many songs, get it out the way. Don't get me twisted, I also know he loved the music, and loved making it, but I think he knew he wasn't going to be here much longer. Pac always used to say he wasn't happy here and he feel his time was coming. That's why he lived so much in the moment of making the music." Personally (and eerily), Tupac seemed to view the record as his transition from one life to another— artistically—explaining just a week before his death that "I've got another album droppin' (in October, 1996) under an alias name, Makaveli. Its called Killuminati…Its not that I idolize this one guy Machiavelli. I idolize that type of thinking where you do whatever's gonna make you achieve your goal…I'm at a point where I'm in charge. I don't have to answer to anybody; I'm in total control…I never thought I was the best rapper…I think I'm the realest nigga out there. I do think that. I think I own that…I'm not the king, I'm not the teacher or nothing like that, but I feel like I don't have no peers."

Before he passed, Tupac had bright hopes for the future, and ever the work-a-holic, had a busy schedule planned for the remainder of 1996 which included "a remix to 'What's Your Phone Number' with all new lyrics. We took that MC Lyte beat from her new song she has out..(Keep On Movin' Up) It's so freaky you won't believe it... I got a whole new album out...waiting for the sound track. It's clean..all positive..all in the vein of songs like 'Keep Your Head Up' and 'Brenda's Got A Baby'. It's that type of stuff. I just put out a hardcore double album.. and next I'm gonna put out an introspective album.. It'll be like a 'Me Against The World pt 2' That's what I think my fans are looking for." Big Syke recalled that he and Tupac had plans for a "Thug Life Vol. 2 album, and it was just gonna be me and him, because wasn't nobody else around at the time that had been in Thug Life. That's where those songs—'My Closest Row Dogs', 'Better Days', that was my song, actually. Johnny J had done the beat, and Pac had heard the song, loved the song, and when you hear that chorus, 'Better Dayz, Better Dayz', that was my song, and Pac liked it and did it over." Among the other items on Tupac's agenda for the future, he and production sidekick Johnny J had plans for what the producer describes as "an independent production company called 'Non-Stop Productions', where we were gonna produce tracks for all kinda genres, from Alanis Morrisette to country artists. I was gonna do the music, and Pac was gonna write the lyrics, and that shit would have been huge too. So I have no regrets, the only thing that hurts me deeply is we didn't get to extend the levels that he was beginning to reach at the time over where we wanted to go musically. Both me and him were ready to take the genres of music to another level, instead of all of it being just straight rap. Its not that he was ready to retire from rap, I just know he was ready to write R&B, and Alternative, or Country music lyrics. He was so bold, and was that fucking dope to where he would say 'Johnny, I'll write the lyrics to whatever song we need to write.' Where he was actually going to write for singers, not just for rappers. I feel bad that we never got to take it to that level, that we never got to realize that together. I think another thing is that we'd recorded such a large catalog of unreleased music by the time he died, that we had touched everything we needed to touch. So creatively we'd definitely reached a peak, and were kind of ready to climb a new creative mountain. I think we were both motivated in that direction in part because we'd kind of gotten bored, I would say so as far as straight rap went. Pac was ready and mature enough as an artist to branch out like that." In terms of where he saw himself by the beginning of the 21st Century, Tupac envisioned himself "being the A&R person and an artist that drop an album like Paul McCartney every five years. Not that I'm like Paul McCartney but there's no rapper who ever did it so that's why I use him as an example. But I wanna do it at leisure. My music will mean something and I'll drop deeper shit. I'll have my own production company which I'm close to right now...I'm doing my own movies. I have my own restaurant...I just wanna expand. I'm starting to put out some calendars for charity. I'm gonna start a little youth league in California so we can start playing some east coast teams..some southern teams...I wanna have like a Pop Warner League except the rappers fund it and they're the head coaches. Have a league where you can get a big trophy with diamonds in it for a nigguh to stay drug free and stay in school. That's the only way you can be on the team. We'll have fun and eat pizza and have the finest girls there and throw concerts at the end of the year. That's what I mean by giving back."

Another close friend and artistic collaborator of Tupac's, Big Syke, viewed the rap icon's death in similar terms as Shakur seemed to—in an artistic context—explaining that "when Pac said 'I might not change the world, but I can bet you I'm gonna spark the brain that will,' that, to me, like certified his death, to where he was like 'I had to die homie, to get these motherfuckers to believe me.' When he said that, I felt like he felt he could go on and die, because he'd fulfilled what he was here to do for the world. He is our Martin Luther King, he is our Malcom X. He's the Black Elvis, and Elvis didn't do nothing but make music. Pac was the Black Jesus, that's how our people look at him. He was a prophet. I think what Pac brung to the whole world is: I'm not the only one feeling like this. And that's why the world's not letting Pac go, kids now is growing up on Tupac, like back when my mama was playing Marvin Gaye. That's him now. Look at that video 'I Am Mad At'cha', he was already hanging out with the legends, he knew where he was headed. The only thing he could do to get any bigger at that point was die. He knew he was a martyr. There wasn't no other way, destiny was already wrote. Cause all our destiny is death, you just got to immortalize yourself while your here with the work you get done in preparation. Then you got enough material there to answer the questions that people are gonna be asking and want to know after you gone. Pac had the catalog to carry his legacy, and I always felt people was naturally willing to follow Pac, with blind faith. If Pac said 'We all goin' down here to jump off this bridge,' there would have been a million motherfuckas lining up to go over. The key with Pac is he wasn't making them blind, he was making them see, that's why they had faith and followed him. Pac answered all the questions that people ever had about themselves. He had this saying: if you don't have nothing to life for, you need to find something to die for. If you got something to die for, you need to find something to live for. And if you go straight to the middle of that like he did, Pac struck that balance, where you got something to live for and something to die for…" Personally, more than he misses working alongside Tupac creatively in the studio, Syke misses "his laugh mostly, even when we was working. Even when we was at the studio, always working, he was always cracking some jokes. That's what I miss the most, just him laughing and shit, kicking it, smoking weed and talking shit. Just his smile, and when he same your name, that right there itself. Just him speaking, his voice, his laughing, that's what I miss. The music part was always the bigger picture of what we was doing, but I'm key on homeboys. I love my homies, whether its the music or not, I'mma still love you. Pac was loyal, but everybody is loyal to something different, and for Pac, I would say above all else he was loyal to his black people, period. It was more than just me, it was a bigger picture, always a bigger picture for him than just his immediate circle; it was his whole clique plus anybody else who came around who was trying to ride in the direction he was going. That's what he was loyal to, and by him being loyal to his people, he couldn't help but be loyal to me, and Napolian, and everybody who was around him. Because the way he was moving, in that direction either you moving or you not."

For his part, producer Shock G seems to measure Tupac's legacy in terms of his work ethic ahead of any other analysis, such that "(Pac was) constantly writing, constantly working—from the studio straight to the set, out of town, straight to the commercial he had to film, back in the studio, straight to those cat's studios he promised he'd go by—doesn't really wanna go over there, but he knows how much it'll mean to them. Tupac Shakur was the hardest working man in hip hop, hands down. His work proves that— since he's died, more work's come out than when he was alive." Among the more anticipated albums to come out in the first few years following Tupac's passing was his official album with the Outlawz, aptly titled 'Still I rise'—one of the first projects to lure Johnny J out of seclusion and back into the studio. Recalling the updating he did to the production of the album, Johnny explains that the experience was "like a Tupac-Outlawz-Johnny J reunion, a real sensitive situation. It had been largely recorded when Pac was alive, but I went in there and restructured it somewhat, beefed it up, flavored some stuff up, and most of those songs ended up scattering out to the posthumous material...When we recorded the additional vocal tracks from the Outlawz for that album, the maturity level for the group had definitely gone up a notch. The growth was unbelievable, and there was magic back in the room again. Pac's spirit was still there, even though we didn't have him there lyrically, his vocals were already recorded and still there pushing everybody. So it was like he was still in the room. And I give the Outlawz all the credit in the world, because their growth as a group elevated things to another level, and it sounded that much better with my production under it. It felt almost like that was the missing link to those guys." Preceding 'Still I Rise', the estate of Tupac Shakur—which now shared ownership of the majority of the so-called 'Makaveli material' with Death Row Records—had released a Greatest Hits LP in collaboration with Death Row, which produced the hit single 'Changes.' Additionally, in November, 1997, Amaru Records had released the first double-LP of post-humous material, entitled 'Are You Still Down (Remember Me?)', combed entirely from pre-Death Row material, and released independent of Knight's involvement or participation. The album—following on the heels of the 4X platinum 'Makaveli', debuted at number 1, and was quickly certified double platinum. Critical reviews of the album were positive overall, and the first glimpse fans and critics alike had gotten of Tupac's back-catalog. *Rolling Stone Magazine's* lengthy review of the album commented that "if you've ever had an enemy, Tupac's bravado can be truly intoxicating, and some of the hate rants here are prime Tupac…'Hellrazor' and 'Fuck All Y'All' are two of his toughest tracks ever: morbid, blustering, brutal…At its best, Tupac's music articulates the mindless rage that's always been part of rock & roll's inspiration. He taps into the same raving, inchoate fury that inspired the Stones' 'Get Off of My Cloud,' the Sex Pistols' 'Bodies' and N.W.A.'s 'Gangsta Gangsta.'" *Vibe Magazine* commented that the double-LP succeeded in giving "hip-hop's complex crown prince…a new voice," while *Spin Magazine*, in an 8 out of 10 rating, called the album "eerie and undeniable…Even after death, 2Pac isn't going gentle into that good night; if this album is any gauge, he's not letting us go either, at least not anytime soon." Entertainment Weekly, in perhaps the most sobering review of the album, commented that the album was "a bittersweet reminder of a gifted…artist lost in the rap wars." In December of 1999, the 2Pac/Outlawz LP debuted at number 1 on the Billboard Top 200 Album Chart and went Platinum, receiving positive critical reviews that included Uncut calling the album "pleasantly diverse", while *The Wire* commented that "in places, Tupac sounds split in two, playing the part of wise father." In November, 2000, a spoken-word album of Tupac poem recitals was released, which was hailed by critics across the board. *Rolling Stone Magazine* commented that the album displayed "a more sensitive Tupac...shining light on a side of (him) that often gets forgotten," while Entertainment Weekly again sunk our collective sails a bit by pointing out that "the rapper's poetry...leaves listeners assured of his (poetic) gifts and saddened by his death." The consensus among critics regarding the first 5 post-humous Tupac releases was universal: that he had worlds more to offer us creatively.

In March of 2001, Amaru/Death Row emerged with yet another posthumous double-LP, entitled 'Until the End of Time', which debuted—as usual—atop the Billboard Top 200 Album chart, moving the usual 2 million copies with little effort, and producing the smash single 'Until the End of Time', set to the 1980s Mr. Mister hit 'Broken Wings.' *Rolling Stone Magazine* commented that "on the better tracks...his keen sense of justice and fidelity —be it of the political or street variety —is at its sharpest." *Entertainment Weekly*, meanwhile, hailed Tupac "at his best...(elevating) gangsta boasts into poetic, sorrow-filled ruminations on thug life." The following year, in November of 2002, 'Better Days' were blessed upon Tupac fans, as the rapper's estate released his seventh posthumous album, which again debuted atop the Billboard Charts and earned its requisite double-platinum certification. Pushed by the hit single 'Thug Mansions', which featured former Tupac-rival Nas. The following year, in December, 2003, a soundtrack to the Tupac-narrated motion picture 'Resurrection', received the same fan treatment as prior post-humous releases had. While the album was comprised of a mix of un-released material and classics from Tupac's catalog, critics found is a pleasant balance of the two, with *Uncut Magazine* calling the release "intense and itchy." In early, 2004, Death Row Records released '2Pac Live', and late that same year, the estate of Tupac Shakur issued what has become the most recent post-humous release, 'Loyal to the Game', produced almost entirely by Eminem as a Christmas bonus for fans. The latter modern-day rap icon categorized this opportunity as that of a career lifetime, explaining that "I just got sent a bunch of Tupac acappellas and went crazy with them..Whatever I could salvage out of anything, I just banged out a bunch of tracks. It's not difficult when you get somebody like Tupac and you already have their vocals. All you gotta do is find the tempo of the song, and you just build the beat around it. That's what I like to do anyway. For two or three weeks straight, we just went at it." This release predictably went platinum, debuting atop the Billboard Top 200 Album Chart, and inspired *Vibe Magazine* to hail the album as "arguably the strongest of 2Pac's posthumous LPs." *Rolling Stone Magazine*, in its review, commented that "Pac's rhymes easily dominate any other sound on the album." The magazine's review comically concluded "see you next year, Pac." For Tupac's listening public to have arrived at the point where they took for granted—as critics sometimes seem to—that every new year would bring a new Tupac album would be arguably the greatest insult to his legacy. It is the artistic consistency and timeless bearing of Shakur's music and message that has kept his catalog in demand to the tune of over 22 million posthumous records sold. Critics aside—it would seem by the fondness with which Tupac's fans receive his new material year after year, that the rapper's relevance remains intact. For his part, Shock G—the man who helped discover Tupac—views Tupac's legacy not in modern terms, but rather in the zone where Tupac was happiest—in the moment of creation—reasoning that "when people say Pac is the best rapper of all time, they don't just mean he's the best rapper, they mean what he had to say was most potent, most relevant, and that he was the better human being. Tupac pulled from Martin Luther King, Malcom X... all the great speakers. Its like pour those words out because you mean it...Pac rapped from the pit of his stomach—Humpty Hump and Slick Rick rhyme from the nasal palette; Nas rhymes from the back of his throat; Pac rhymed from the pit of his stomach. He was singing it, singing it out. So if you listen to it, there wasn't many rappers doing that...If you want to mourn, do it for your own personal loss. Don't mourn for 'Pac, remember him for his art and don't be sad for his death. 'Pac lived a short, fast, concentrated, an intense life. He lived a 70 year life in 25 years. He went out the way he wanted: in the glitter of the fast life, hit record on the charts, new movie in the can, and money in the pocket. All 'Pac wanted was to hear himself on the radio and see himself on the movie screen. He did all that—and more."

Everyone has an opinion on why the resonance of Tupac's music remains so commercially and socially potent. Tupac's close friend and musical muse Johnny J argues—without hesitation—that "the music Pac made—almost 10 years ago—is relevant now more than ever. Very necessary to be in this game right now." *Rolling Stone Magazine*, in attempting to pinpoint why Tupac became hip hop's artistic pinnacle, has surmised that "the key to Tupac's appeal was how vividly he dramatized the tension between his Thug Life and his moments of tenderness." Suge Knight, meanwhile, seems to focus more on the success Tupac achieved in such a short time as perhaps his greatest single achievement in context of securing legacy, pointing out that "September 7th, (1996) is...a sad day. Its an educational day...Tupac took Death Row to the next level. I mean, we worked hard, we laid the foundation down, Snoop took the baton and he ran with it...But when Tupac got the baton, not only did he win the race, he finished so fast hc (was) able to sit back and drink some thug passion, and come up with another play." Fellow musician and co-star of 'Poetic Justice', speaking for the female faction of Tupac's massive fan base, sees Tupac's longevity as more simply a matter of his being the first to say "that ill shit that niggas be thinking and on one wanted to say." For all the voices that spoke after him on behalf of the hip hop generation—from 50 Cent to Jay Z to Eminem—all bow down and pay homage to the golden path Tupac laid for hip hop into modern dominance over pop culture. This is particularly true of the Eminem, who openly idolizes Tupac, and seems to see the key to his lasting omnipresence in rap—from a decade ago to modern day—as simply a matter of his "personality. I guess no matter what color you was or where you came from, you felt like you could relate to him. He made you feel like you knew him. I think that honestly, Tupac was the greatest songwriter that ever lived. He made it seem so easy. The emotion was there, and feeling, and everything he was trying to describe. You saw a picture that he was trying to paint. That's what I picked up from him, making your words so vivid that somebody can picture them in their head." In the annals of hip hop, it can be argued you will not find a harder martyr or more loyal partner than Tupac was to anyone who was willing to ride his **Underground Railroad** out into a **Thug Life** that he lived as an **Outlaw** immortalized by his struggle on behalf of a generation millions-strong. The very magnitude of Tupac's catalog of work is a testament to the measure of his sacrifice. Perhaps the greatest success of Shakur's body of work in sum is the fact that it has seemingly evolved in both appeal and impact to a point beyond even Tupac's own boldest expectations in his lifetime: "My music is not for everyone. It's only for the strong-willed, the (street) soldiers music. It's not like party music—I mean, you could gig to it, but it's spiritual. My music is spiritual. It's like Negro spirituals, except for the fact that I'm not saying 'We shall Overcome.' I'm saying that we are overcome…And the raps that I'm rappin to my community shouldn't be filled with rage? They shouldn't be filled with same atrocities that they gave me? The media they don't talk about it, so in my raps I have to talk about it, and it seems foreign because there's no one else talking about it…My raps are a decision, rabble rousing, spiritual, like gospel music. I don't want to dance. We have so many things to deal with, we need to talk straight up and down…I feel as though anything I rap about, shit anybody can check my card on it. And I gotta be able to show and prove whenever anybody wanna pull my card on it…As long as they got bullets and 2-inch tape, there will be justice out this motherfucker."

Discography/Chart History:

15.) 'Loyal to the Game'
Amaru/Interscope
Released: December 14, 2004
Highest Chart Position: # 1 on the Billboard Top 200 Album Chart and R&B/Hip Hop Chart
Certified: Platinum

14.) '2Pac Live'
Death Row/Koch
Released: August 6, 2004
Highest Chart Position: # 46 on the Billboard Top 200 Album Chart

13.) '2Pac Resurrection'—The Original Motion Picture Soundtrack
Interscope Records
Released: November 11, 2003
Highest Chart Position: # 1 on the Billboard Top 200 Album Chart and R&B/Hip Hop Chart
Certified: Platinum

12.) 'Better Dayz' (Double LP)
Interscope/Amaru/Death Row Records
Released: November 26, 2002
Highest Chart Position: # 1 on the Billboard Top 200 Album Chart and R&B/Hip Hop Chart
Certified: 2x Platinum

11.) 'Until the End of Time' (Double LP)
Amaru/Death Row/Interscope Records
Released: March 27, 2001
Highest Chart Position: # 1 on the Billboard Top 200 Album Chart and
R&B/Hip Hop Chart
Certified: 3x Platinum

10.) 'The Rose That Grew From Concrete'
Amaru/Interscope Records
Released: November 21, 2000

9.) '2Pac and the Outlawz: Still I Rise'
Amaru/Jive, Interscope/Death Row Records
Released: December 14, 1999
Highest Chart Position: # 7 on the Billboard Top 200 Album Chart,
and # 2 on the R&B/Hip Hop Chart
Certified: 2x Platinum

8.) '2Pac: Greatest Hits' (Double LP)
Amaru/Jive, Interscope/Death Row Records
Released: November 24, 1998
Highest Chart Position: # 1 on the Billboard Top 200 Album Chart and
R&B/Hip Hop Album Chart
Certified: 9x Platinum

7.) 'R U Still Down (Remember Me?)' (Double LP)
Amaru/Jive Records
Released: November 25, 1997
Highest Chart Position: # 1 on the Billboard Top 200 Album Chart and
R&B/Hip Hop Album Chart
Certified: 4x Platinum

6.) 'Makaveli: The Don Killimunati: The 7 Day Theory'
Death Row Records
Released: November 5, 1996
Highest Chart Position: # 1 on the Billboard Top 200 Album Chart and
R&B/Hip Hop Album Chart
Certified 4x Platinum

5.) 'All Eyez on Me' (Double LP)
Death Row Records
Released: February 13, 1996
Highest Chart Position: # 1 on the Billboard Top 200 Album Chart and
R&B/Hip Hop Album Chart
Certified 9x Platinum

4.) 'Me Against the World'
Interscope Records
Released: February 27, 1995
Highest Chart Position: # 1 on the Billboard Top 200 Album Chart and
R&B/Hip Hop Album Chart
Certified 2x Platinum

3.) 'Thug Life Vol. One'
Interscope Records
Released: September 26, 1994
Highest Chart Position: # 42 on the Billboard Top 200 Album Chart
and # 6 on the R&B/Hip Hop Chart
Certified: Platinum

2.) 'Strictly 4 My N.I.G.G.A.Z.'
Interscope Records
Released: February 1, 1993
Highest Chart Position:
Certified: Platinum

1.) '2Pacalypse Now'
Interscope Records
Released: November 12, 1991
Highest Chart Position: # 64 on the Billboard Top 200 Album Chart
and # 4 on the R&B/Hip Hop Chart
Certified: Platinum

About the Author

Jake Brown resides in Nashville, Tennessee and is President of Versailles Records. An avid writer, Jake has penned several books, including Colossus Books' best-sellers: *Your Body's Calling Me: The Life and Times of Robert "R" Kelly — Music, Love, Sex & Money; Ready to Die: the Story of Biggie Smalls — Notorious B.I.G.; 50 Cent: No Holds Barred and Jay-Z and the Roc-a-Fella Dynasty.* Other published titles by Jake Brown include: *An Education in Rebellion: The Biography of Nikki Sixx* and *Dust N' Bones: The Untold Story of Izzy Stradlin.*

ORDER FORM

WWW.AMBERBOOKS.COM

Fax Orders: 480-283-0991   Telephone Orders: 480-460-1660
Postal Orders: Send Checks & Money Orders to:
    Amber Books
    1334 E. Chandler Blvd., Suite 5-D67, Phoenix, AZ 85048
Online Orders: E-mail: Amberbk@aol.com

_____ *Tupac Shakur—(2Pac) In The Studio*, $16.95
_____ *Jay-Z…and the Roc-A-Fella Dynasty*, $16.95
_____ *Your Body's Calling Me: The Life & Times of "Robert" R. Kelly*, $16.95
_____ *Ready to Die: Notorious B.I.G.*, $16.95
_____ *Suge Knight: The Rise, Fall, and Rise of Death Row Records*, $21.95
_____ *50 Cent: No Holds Barred*, $16.95
_____ *Aaliyah—An R&B Princess in Words and Pictures* ,$10.95
_____ *You Forgot About Dre: Dr. Dre & Eminem*, $10.95
_____ *Divas of the New Millenium*, $16.95
_____ *Michael Jackson: The King of Pop*, $29.95
_____ *The House that Jack Built (Hal Jackson Story)*, $16.95

Name:_____

Company Name:_____

Address:_____

City:_____State:_____Zip:_____

Telephone: (____) _____E-mail:_____

For Bulk Rates Call: **480-460-1660**   # ORDER NOW

Tupac Shakur	$16.95
Jay-Z…	$16.95
Your Body's Calling Me:	$16.95
Ready to Die: Notorious B.I.G.,	$16.95
Suge Knight:	$21.95
50 Cent: No Holds Barred,	$16.95
Aaliyah—An R&B Princess	$10.95
Dr. Dre & Eminem	$10.95
Divas of the New Millenium,	$16.95
Michael Jackson: The King of Pop	$29.95
The House that Jack Built	$16.95

❑ Check ❑ Money Order ❑ Cashiers Check
❑ Credit Card: ❑ MC ❑ Visa ❑ Amex ❑ Discover

CC#_____

Expiration Date:_____

Payable to:
    Amber Books
    1334 E. Chandler Blvd., Suite 5-D67
    Phoenix, AZ 85048

Shipping: $5.00 per book. Allow 7 days for delivery.
Sales Tax: Add 7.05% to books shipped to Arizona addresses.

Total enclosed: $_____